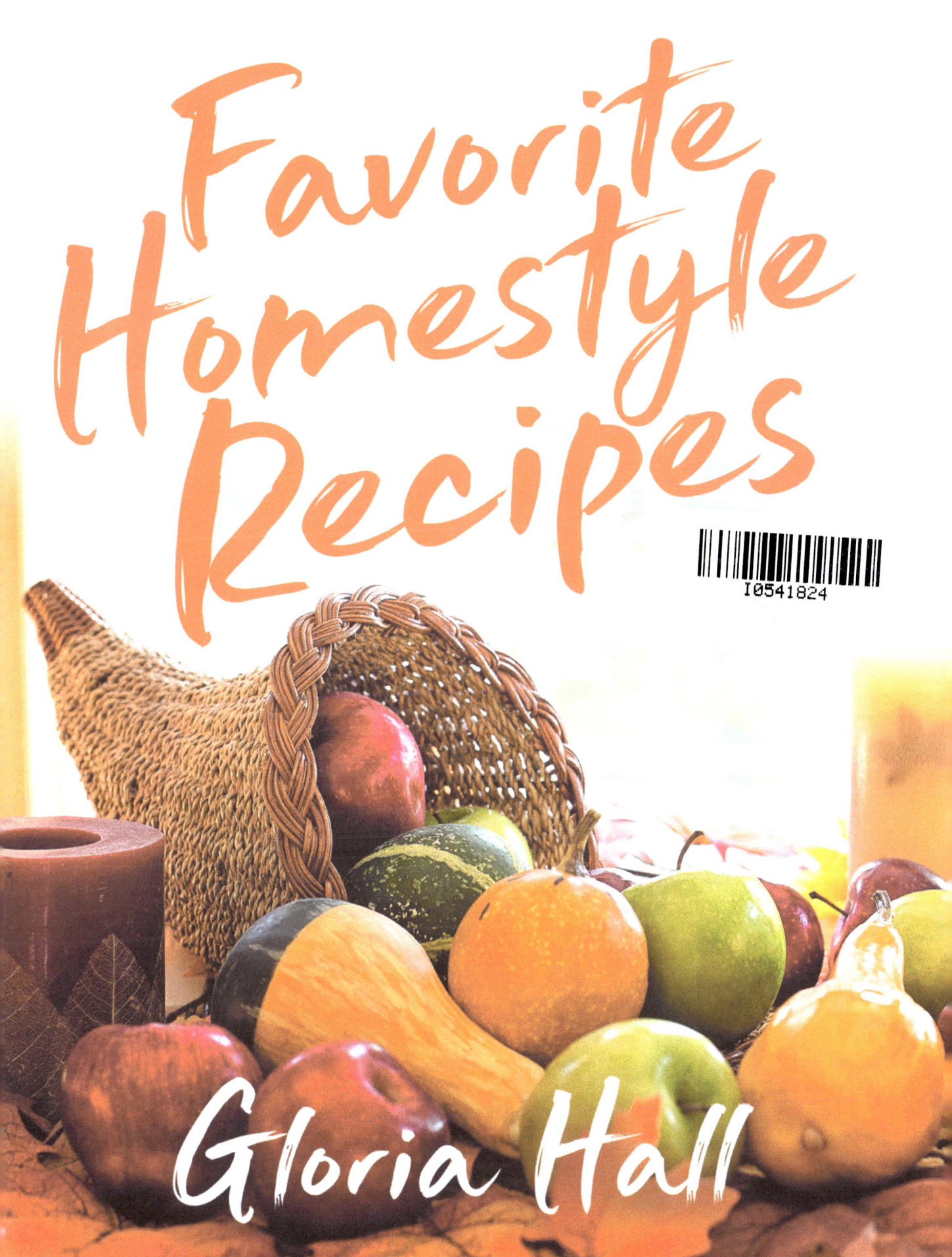

Favorite Homestyle Recipes

Gloria Hall

I0541824

ISBN 978-1-957943-49-7 (paperback)
ISBN 978-1-957943-50-3 (digital)

Rushmore Press LLC
1 800 460 9188
www.rushmorepress.com

Printed in the United States of America

Dedication

I cheerfully dedicate this book to all people who love to cook and even to those who only cook and even to those who only cook out of necessity, for I have endeavored to include something for everyone.

Many of us today often find it necessary to opt for fast food because of our busy schedules. But we refuse to place the "closed" sign above the kitchen door. And we still manage to whip up mouth-watering dishes for our families.

Some of the recipes I have included are my own creations, some I have included are my own creations, some I have modified, and some are treasured Family keepsakes: however, they all reflect the love of good cooking. And I hope that you will enjoy them as much as I do.

As a person who enjoys being in the kitchen, I don't need much motivation to be found there making my favorite fudge to give as a gift or turning out a steaming casserole for a church potluck.

My job as a court report is interesting and rewarding, but sometimes requires me to work long hours, thereby leaving little time for cooking.

But I love the challenge. And whether I'm being creative or relying on a favorite family recipe, I get satisfaction from knowing homemade food is so appreciated because it adds a personal touch and says "I care."

May you and your family be delighted with the recipes that follow.

Gloria Hall

O taste and see that the Lord is good: blessed is the man that trusteth in Him.

Home is not a house alone,
It's family and friends…
The warmth that kitchen gatherings
And a cup of cup of coffee lends.

It's love and understanding
Blended well with kindliness,
That fills the heat and makes the home
A place of happiness.

Beverly C. Willard

HEALTH AND MONEY—

Between these two temporal blessings is this difference:
Money is the most envied but the least enjoyed.
Health is the most enjoyed, but the least envied.

Adapted from Colton

Table of Contents

Appetizers, Relishes & Pickles

Appetizers

Appetizers are those treats that can be served either at the start of a meal or at a reception or open house. Listed below are quick appetizers that can be served anytime with crackers, thin sliced toasted bread or potato chips:

1. Caviar flavored with onion juice.
2. Cream cheese with chopped chutney and dash of curry powder.
3. Labster tail moistened with lemon juice.
4. Almonds or pecans roasted and chopped, then mixed with anchovy paste.
5. Cream cheese with chopped pickle.
6. Chicken livers minced and moistened with mayonnaise.
7. Cheese squares with olive attached by toothpick.
8. Liverwurst with pistachio nuts.
9. Sardines with caviar paste.
10. Minced eggs with anchovies.
11. Cream cheese and horseradish.
12. Cream cheese and anchovy paste with grated onion.
13. Herring squares mashed in its own juice with dash of vinegar and Tabasco sauce.
14. Peanut butter and bacon toasted on dark bread.
15. Deviled ham with chopped onions and Spanish olives.
16. Stilton cheese moistened with port wine.
17. Shrimp flavored with French dressing.
18. Caviar mixed with cream cheese with dash of Worcestershire sauce.
19. Peanuts roasted, crushed and mixed with anchovy paste.
20. Sardine slices toped with chopped olives.
21. Pimento cheese mixed with a dash of horseradish.
22. Minced shrimp with onion juice.
23. Cream cheese with dash of Worcestershire sauce and chives.

CHEESE BALL

1 lb. Cheddar cheese, grated
1 (8 ¼ oz.) small can crushed
Pineapple, drained (save juice)

1 Tbsp. mayonnaise
½ tsp. dry mustard
½ c. walnuts

Combine first 4 ingredients and mix thoroughly with a fork. Add some pineapple juice, if necessary, to make mixture soft and moist enough to handle.

Form a large ball and roll in walnuts until completely coated. Serve with whole grain crackers.

TORTILLA-WRAPPED CHILE RELLENOS

oil (for deep frying)
3 (4 oz.) cans whole green chilies
10 oz. Cheddar cheese
10 large flour tortillas (10-inch diameter)
1/2c. Milk

1 egg
1 c. all-purpose flour
1 ½ tsp. chili powder
1/2tsp. garlic salt
salsa

Separate chilies to make 10 individual pieces. Slice cheese into 1o strips. Place cheese pieces inside chilies. Place cheese-stuffed chilies in center of each tortilla. Fold ends of tortillas over chilies, envelope-style. Secure with toothpicks.

In small bowl, beat milk and egg until blended. Lightly spoon flour into measuring cup; level off. In small bowl, combine flour, chili powder and garlic salt. Dip tortilla in egg mixture. Coat with flour mixture.

In deep fat fryer or heavy saucepan, fry tortillas in 3 inches hot oil for 2 minutes on each side or until golden brown. Serve with salsa. Makes 10 chili rellenos.

Recipe

Page Number

Soups, Salads & Sauces

Salads

Additions and Garnishes

Slice hard-cooked eggs
Radished
Chopped green or ripe olives
Nut meats
Pimento
Green pepper
Sardines
Anchovles
Slivered cheeses
Julienned ham
Chicken
Grated carrots
Cubed celery
Onions—pickled, grated or
Pearl onions
Tomatoes, sliced and dipped in Finely chopped
    parsley or chives
Capers
Dwarf tomatoes stuffed with Cottage cheese
Fresh herbs—springs or chopped
Mint leaves
Cooked beets cut into shapes Or sticks
Lemon slices with pinked edges And dipped in
    chopped parsley
Raw cauliflower

Tips for Tossed Salads

Always handle salad greens with care.

Wash well, drain and dry greens before storing; chili well before using.

To core lettuce, smack head stem end down on counter top. Then Twist the core out.

It is better to tear greens into bite-sized pieces to avoid bruising with knife.

Don't cut up tomatoes for a tossed salad since their juices thin the dressing and wilt the greens.

Use them only for garnishing the salad bowl.

Select only firm, hard, and green cucumbers. The skin should have a slight sheen, but if it is highly polished, it is probably waxed and the skin should be removed.

Use wild greens such as dandelion, sorrel or winter cress for a different flavor and texture in tossed salads.

About Potato Salad

Potato salad is best made from Potatoes cooked in their jackets and peeled and marinated while Still warm. Small red waxy Potatoes hold their shape when Sliced or diced and do not absorb an excessive amount of dressing or become mushy.

Soup Accompaniments

Clear Soups—crisp crackers, cheese pastry, cheese-spread toast strips.

Cream Soups—cheese popcorn, seeded crackers, pretzels, pickles and olives.

Chowders and Meat Soups—Melba toast, sour pickles, oyster Crackers, bread sticks, relishes, toasted garlic bread.

☐ SOUPS, SALADS & SAUCES

CARROT AND APPLE SALAD

1 Large apple
2 c. coarsely shredded carrot
½ c. raisins
½ (3 oz.) pkg. cream cheese

½ c. mayonnaise
1 Tbsp. orange juice
ground nutmeg

Core and slice apple. In a mixing bowl, combine apple, shredded Carrot and raisins.

To make dressing, in a small bowl, beat cream cheese until fluffy. Stir in mayonnaise or salad dressing and orange juice.

Spoon dressing over apple-carrot mixture. Toss mixture to coat with dressing. Sprinkle lightly with nutmeg. Cover and chill until serving time. Makes 4 servings.

APPLE AND RAISIN SALAD

5 red, tart, juicy apples
½ c. raisins
½ tsp. lemon juice

½ c. mayonnaise
lettuce

Wash, but do not peel, apples; core and dice. Immediately toss with raisins, lemon juice and mayonnaise. Pile lightly into lettuce cups on individual Salad plates. One-half cup cubed Cheddar cheese may be added. Makes 5 servings.

COMPANY SALAD

1 (6 oz.) pkg. lemon jell-0
3 ½ c. hot water
1 c. pecans
1 c. pineapple juice
3 bananas, sliced
1 ½ c. miniature marshmallows

1 c. pineapple juice
1 ½ Tbsp. flour
½ c. sugar
1 egg, beaten
1 ½ pt. whipped cream

Dissolve Jell-O in hot water; cool. Add pineapple, bananas, nuts and marshmallows. Chill to set.

Heat pineapple juice. Combine flour, sugar and egg and mix with Pineapple Juice. Cook, stirring constantly, until thickened. Cool. Fold in Whipped cream and spread over jell-o. Will keep for several days in refrigerator.

COTTAGE CHEESE SALAD

1 small carton cottage cheese
1 regular pkg. dry Jell-O (any
Flavor)

1 (8 oz.) can crushed pineapple,
drained
1 regular carton Cool Whip

Mix dry Jell-O into cottage cheese. Add drained pineapple and Stir in Cool Whip. Let stand in refrigerator for several hours.

FROZEN CRANBERRY-BANANA SALAD

1 (20 oz.) can pineapple tidbis
5 medium firm bananas, halved
Lengthwise and sliced
1 (16 oz.) can whole-berry
Cranberry sauce

½ c. sugar
1 (12 oz.) carton frozen whipped
topping, thawed
½ c. chopped walnuts

Drain Pineapple juice into a medium bowl; set pineapple aside. Add bananas to the Juice. In a large bowl, combine cranberry sauce and sugar. Remove bananas, discarding juice, and add to cranberry mixture. Stir in pineapple, whipped topping and nuts.

Pour into a 13x9x2-inch dish. Freeze until solid. Remove from the freezer 15 minutes before Cutting.

FLUFFY FRUIT SALAD

2 (20 oz. each) cans crushed
Pineapple
2/3 c. sugar
2 Tbsp. all-purpose flour
2 eggs, slightly beaten
¼ c. orange juice
3 Tbsp. lemon juice

1 Tbsp. vegetable oil
2 (17 oz. each) cans fruit
cocktail, drained
2 (11 oz. each) cans mandarin
oranges, drained
2 bananas, sliced
1 c. heavy cream, whipped

Drain pineapple, reserving 1 cup juice in a small saucepan. Set pineapple aside.

To saucepan, add sugar, flour, eggs, orange juice, lemon juice and oil. Bring to a boil, stirring constantly. Boil for 1 minute. Remove from the heat and let cool.

In a salad bowl, combine the pineapple, fruit cocktail, oranges and bananas. Fold in whipped cream and cooled sauce. Chill for several hours.

HEAVENLY FRUIT SALAD

1 (3 ½ OZ.) box Jell-O Instant
Vanilla pudding
1 (8 oz.) can pineapple chunks
and juice

½ pt. whipping cream, whipped
2 c. small marshmallows
1 small can Mandarin oranges
2 small bananas, sliced

Mix cream and pudding. Add pineapple. Stir in marshmallows, oranges and bananas. Chill and serve. Serves 6 to 8.

7-UP SALAD

2 (3 oz.) pkg. lemon Jell-O
2 c. 7-Up
1 can crushed pineapple

2 large bananas, sliced
1 c. mini marshmallows
½ c. shredded cheese

Topping:

½ c. sugar
2 Tbsp. flour
1 c. pineapple juice

1 egg, beaten slightly
2 Tbsp. butter
1 c. Dream Whip

Dissolve Jell-O in 1 ¾ cups hot water. Stir in 7-Up. Chill to partially set. Drain pineapple, saving juice. Fold in pineapple, bananas and marshmallows. Chill until firm. Frost with prepared topping. Sprinkle with shredded cheese.

Topping: Combine sugar and flour in pan. Stir in pineapple juice. If necessary, stir a little water into the juice to make 1 cup. Stir in beaten egg. Cook over low heat until it thickens.

Remove from heat and add butter. Cool and chill. Fold in Dream Whip.

LEMONY FRUIT SALAD

3 ¼ OZ. pkg. lemon pudding and
Pie filling mix (not instant)
½ c. sugar
¼ c. water
2 egg yolks
2 c. water
1 c. whipping cream, whipped

29 oz. can peach slices, drained
20 oz. can pineapple chunks,
drained
16 oz. can mandarin oranges,
drained
16 oz. can pear slices, drained

In medium saucepan, combine pudding mix, sugar and ¼ cup water. Stir in egg yolks. Add 2 cups water; mix well. Cook over medium heat until mixture comes to a full boil, stirring constantly. Cool completely.

Fold in whipped cream. Gently fold in drained fruits. Cover Refrigerate several hours or overnight.

PINEAPPLE—LIME VELVET

1 pkg. lime-flavored gelatin
1 c. boiling water
3 oz. pkg. cream cheese
2/3 c. crushed pineapple with juice

½ c. finely cut celery
½ c. heavy cream, whipped
watercress
maraschino cherries

Add gelatin to water and stir until dissolved. Add cheese and beat with a rotary beater until cheese is well blended. Chill until slightly congealed, then add pineapple and celery. Fold in whipped cream lightly, but thorough.

Turn into 4-cup mold that has been rinsed with cold water. Chill until firm. Unmold. Serve on watercress. Garnish with cherries.

TURKEY-APPLE SALAD

1 c. turkey, cut in chunks
3.4 c. chopped apple
½ c. sliced celery

2 Tbsp. raisins
1/3 c. prepared Italian dressing
1 Tbsp. brown sugar

In medium bowl, gently stir together turkey, apple, celery and raisins. In cup, stir together dressing and brown sugar; pour over turkey mixture. Toss gently to coat. Serve on lettuce leaves. Makes 2 servings.

OLD-FASHIONED SWEET COLESLAW

1 small cabbage, finely chopped
2 carrots, shredded
1/3 c. mayonnaise

1 Tbsp. sugar
½ tsp. salt
¼ tsp. pepper

Combine cabbage and carrots. Combine mayonnaise and remaining ingredients. Toss mayonnaise mixture with cabbage mixture. Cover and chill. Makes 6 to 8 servings.

SHREDDED CHICKEN SALAD

3 chicken breasts, cooked and
Shredded

2 oz. pkg. wonton skins, fried
lightly in oil
1 head lettuce, shredded

Dressing:

2 Tbsp. sugar
1 tsp. salt
½ tsp. black pepper

¼ c. salad oil
1 Tbsp. sesame oil
¾ c. Japanese vinegar

TROPICAL CHICKEN SALAD

2 c. cubed, cooked chicken
1 c. chopped celery
1 c. mayonnaise
½ to 1 tsp. curry powder
1 (20 pz.) can chunk pineapple,
Drained

2 large, firm bananas, sliced
1 (11 oz.) can mandarin oranges,
drained
½ c. flaked coconut
¾ c. salted peanuts or cashew
halves

Place chicken and celery in a large bowl. Combine mayonnaise and curry powder; add to chicken mixture and mix well. Cover and chill for at least 30 minutes,
Before serving, add the pineapple, bananas, oranges and coconut; toss gently. Serve on salad greens, if desired. Sprinkle with nuts.

GERMAN POTATO SALAD

5 bacon strips	¼ c. sugar
¾ c. chopped onion	1 tsp, salt
2 Tbsp. all-purpose flour	1/8 tsp. pepper
2/3 c. cider vinegar	6 c. sliced, cooked, peeled
1 1/3 c. water	potatoes

In large skillet, fry bacon until crisp; remove and set aside. Drain all but 2 to 3 tablespoons of drippings, cook onion until tender. Stir in flour, blend well. Add vinegar and water; cook and stir until bubbly and slightly thick. Add sugar and stir until it dissolves.

Crumble bacon; gently stir in bacon and potatoes. Heat through, stirring lightly to coat potato slices. Serve warm.

GERMAN POTATO SALAD AND BRATS

4 slices bacon	½ c. milk
¼ c. sliced green onions	1 ½ s. Hungry Jack mashed
1 ½ c. water	1 ½ c. Hungry Jack mashed
1 ½ c. water	potato flakes
1 beef bouillon cube	5 bratwurst

Dressing:

1 egg, beaten	½ tsp. dry mustard
2 Tbsp. sugar	¼ tsp. celery seed
2 Tbsp. vinegar	1/8 tsp. pepper

In small saucepan, combine all dressing ingredients. Cook over medium heat, stirring constantly, until thickened. Set aside.

In large skillet, fry bacon until crisp. Remove bacon from pan; crumble and set aside. Add onions to bacon drippings and cook until tender. Stir in water and beef bouillon. Bring to rolling boil. Remove from heat. Add milk and potato flakes, stirring until combined. Add bacon and dressing; stir until well mixed. Keep hot.

Grill bratwurst until thoroughly cooked. Split each bratwurst lengthwise, not cutting through completely. Spread open. Top each with about ½ cup hot potato mixture. Serve immediately. Makes 6 servings.

ZESTY SHRIMP AND RICE SALAD

10 oz. PKG. Green Giant Rice
Originals frozen rice medley
1 c. cooked shrimp
¼ c. chopped celery

1 Tbsp. finely chopped onion
2 Tbsp. mayonnaise
1 Tbsp. lemon juice

Place unopened rice pouch in vigorously boiling water in saucepan. Do not cover. Bring water to a second vigorous boil and heat for 16 minutes.

Meanwhile, in medium bowl, combine shrimp, celery, onion, salad dressing and lemon juice. Stir in rice. Chill at least 2 hours before serving.

SOUTHERN-STYLE BARBECUE SAUCE

1 Tbsp. margarine
¼ c. minced onion
1 c. tomato sauce (9 oz.)
1 c. molasses
¼ c. cider vinegar
2 Tbsp. prepared mustard

1 Tbsp. lemon juice
1 tsp. chili powder
½ c. ketchup
1 tsp. salt
1 tsp. pepper
4 Tbsp. Worcestershire sauce

In saucepan, melt margarine over medium heat. Add onion; sauté 3 minutes. Add remaining ingredients. Simmer gently 20 minutes. Can be used on all types of meat. Makes 3 cups.

TEXAS BARBECUE SAUCE

2 medium-sized onions, finely
Chopped
1 clove garlic, finely chopped
1/3 c. vegetable oil
2 Tbsp. chill powder
2 c. catsup
1 Tbsp. celery seed, crushed

¼ c. Worcestershire sauce
½ c. lemon juice
½ c. packed brown sugar
2 Tbsp. prepared mustard
1 c. cider vinegar
2 Tbsp. butter

Sauté onions and garlic in oil in a large saucepan until golden brown and tender, about 1 minutes. Stir in chili powder and cook for one minute. Add all remaining ingredients, except butter. Bring to boiling. Lower heat: simmer, uncovered, stirring often, for 30 minutes. Stir in butter.

— • YOUR FAVORITE RECIPES •—

Recipe

Page Number

14

SOUPS, SALADS & SAUCES

Meats & Main Dishes

Meat Cooking Chart

Roasting	Weight	Minutes Per lb.	Oven Temp.	Internal Temp.
FRESH PORK				
Rib and loin	3-7 lbs	30-40	325	175 F
Leg	5 lbs	25-30	325	170 F
Picnic shoulder	5-10 lbs	40	325	175 F
Shoulder, butt	3-10 lbs	40-50	325	170 F
Boned and rolled				
Shoulder	3-6 lbs	60	325	170 F
BEEF				
Standing ribs – rare	3-7 lbs	25	325	135 F
* medium	3-7 lbs	30	325	165 F
* well done	3-7 lbs	35	325	170 F

For rolled and boned roasts, increase cooking time to 5 to 12 minutes.

	Weight	Minutes Per lb.	Oven Temp.	Internal Temp.
LAMB				
Shoulder * well done	4-10 lbs	40	325	190 F
* boned and rolled	3-6 lbs	40	325	182 F
Leg * medium	5-10 lbs	40	325	175 F
* well done	3-6 lbs	40-50	325	182 F
Crown * well done	3-6 lbs	40-50	325	182 F
SMOKED PORK				
Shoulder and picnic hams	5 lbs	30-40	325	170 F
	8 lbs	30-40	325	175 F
Boneless bull	2 lbs	40	325	180 F
	4 lbs	25	325 F	170 F
Ham	12-20 lbs	16-18	325 F	170 F
	Under 10 lbs	20	325	175 F
	Half hams	25	325	170 F
VEAL				
Loin	4-6 lbs	35	325 F	175 F
Leg	5-10 lbs	35	325	175 F
Boneless	4-10 lbs	45	325 F	175 F
Poultry				
Chicken	3-5 lbs	40	325 F	170 F
Stuffed	over 5 lbs	30	325	170 F
Turkey	8-10 lbs	20	325	175 F
	18-20 lbs	14	325	175 F
Duck	5-10 lbs	30	325	175 F

❑ MEATS & MAIN DISHES

MACARONI BAKE

1 lb. ground beef
½ c. chopped onion
1 can tomato paste
½ tsp. salt
½ tsp. cinnamon
¼ c. flour
½ c. mayonnaise

2 c. milk
2 eggs
½ c. grated Parmesan cheese
¼ tsp. nutmeg
8 oz. pkg. macaroni, cooked and
drained

Brown beef and onion; drain fat, Stir in next 3 ingredients; set aside. Combine flour and mayonnaise; gradually stir in milk. Cook and stir over medium heat until sauce is thick. Do not boil. Beat egg, cheese, and nutmeg together. Gradually stir into sauce. Add macaroni.

Spoon half macaroni mixture into 2-quart oblong baking dish. Cover with meat mixture. Top with remaining macaroni. Bake at 325o for 45 minutes or until set.

FANCY BEEF AND RICE DINNER

1 lb. beef top loin steak
6 green onions, sliced
Into ½-inch lengths
3 Tbsp. butter or margarine
¼ tsp. salt

1/8 tsp. pepper
½ c. dairy sour cream
2 tsp. all-purpose flour
hot, cooked rice

Thinly slice beef into bite-sized strips; set aside, in a 10-inch skillet, cook onions in 1 tablespoon butter or margarine until tender, but not brown. Remove and set aside.

Add 2 tablespoons butter or margarine to skillet. Add half of the beef. Cook quickly over high heat, stirring frequently, for 2 to 3 minutes or until done. Remove beef from skillet. Repeat with remaining beef.

Return all meat to skillet. Stir salt, pepper and green onions into meat. Bring to boiling; reduce heat. Stir together sour cream and flour; stir into meat mixture. Cook and stir until heated through. Do not boil.

Serve meat mixture over hot, cooked rice. Garnish with parsley. Makes 4 servings.

EASY ONE DISH SUPPER

½ loaf frozen white bread dough,
Thawed (1 lb. size)
1 ½ lb. lean ground beef
¼ c. chopped onions
1 can sliced mushrooms, drained
1 (8 oz.) can tomato sauce
2 Tbsp. catsup
1 beef bouillon cube

¼ tsp. oregano
¼ tsp. thyme
¼ tsp. basil
¼ tsp. parsley
1/8 tsp. black pepper
1 egg, beaten
bacon flavored bits

Brown beef and onions in skillet; drain, if necessary. Add next 9 ingredients. Cover. Simmer 15 minutes. Remove from stove and cool to warm.

Divide dough into 20 pieces and place on top of warm beef mixture. Cover with clean towel and let rise 30 minutes or until pieces of bread dough have doubled in size.

Lightly brush dough with beaten egg. Sprinkle with bacon flavored bits. Bake, uncovered, at 375o for 25 to 30 minutes. Makes 8 servings.

QUICK AND EASY SPAGHETTI

1 lb. ground pork or ground beef
1 large carrot, chopped
1 tsp. cornstarch
1 (15 oz.) can sliced mushrooms,
1 (4 oz) can sliced mushrooms,
Drained
1 tsp. dried oregano, crushed

1 tsp. Worcestershire sauce
½ tsp. sugar
½ tsp. dried basil, crushed
¼ tsp. garlic powder
¼ tsp, salt
hot, cooked spaghetti
grated Parmesan cheese

In a 3-quart saucepan, cook the ground pork or ground beef and carrot until the meat is browned. Drain off fat, Stir in cornstarch. Add tomato sauce, mushrooms, oregano, Worcestershire, sugar, basil, garlic powder and salt. Bring mixture to boiling; reduce heat. Simmer, uncovered, about 15 minutes, stirring occasionally.

Serve over hot, cooked spaghetti. Sprinkle on grated Parmesan cheese. Makes 6 servings.

IMPOSSIBLE CHEESEBURGER PIE

1 lb. ground beef
1 c. chopped onion
½ tsp. salt
1 c. shredded Cheddar cheese

1 c. milk
½ c. Bisquick baking mix
2 eggs

Cook ground beef and onion; drain. Stir in salt. Spread in greased 9-inch pie plate. Sprinkle with cheese. Stir remaining ingredients with fork until blended; pour into plate.

Bake 25 minutes or until knife inserted in center comes out clean. Makes 8 servings.

CHILI RELLENOS CASSEROLE

1 LB. Cheddar and Jack cheeses
1 small can evaporated milk
1 can whole Ortega chiles
1 lb. hamburger
4 Tbsp. flour

4 to 5 eggs
½ tsp. salt
½ tsp. pepper
½ tsp. chili powder
1 medium can tomato sauce

Butter 9 x 12-inch casserole pan. Grate cheeses and save one cup. Lay chiles on bottom. Brown hamburger and drain. Put meat on chiles, then layer two cheeses on top of meat. Beat eggs, milk, flour, salt, pepper, and chili powder together; pour over top.

Bake 35 minutes in 375° oven until brown and firm. Remove from oven. Pour tomato sauce on Top and remaining cheeses. Return to oven 5 to 7 minutes to melt cheese. Let stand 5 to 10 minutes before serving.

COTTAGE MEAT LOAF

2 lb. lean ground beef

½ c. tomato ketchup

1/3 c. tomato juice

½ tsp. salt

½ ts. Pepper

1.8 tsp. red pepper

2 tsp. prepared mustard

1/2 c. finely chopped onions

¾ c fresh breadcrumbs

2 eggs, beaten

Topping:

¼ c. tomato ketchup

2 tsp. brown sugar

½ tsp. prepared mustard

In large bowl, combine ketchup, tomato juice, salt, black and red peppers, eggs, breadcrumbs, onions, and mustard. Mix until thoroughly, blended, Add ground beef. Mix gently, but thoroughly.

Line a 9 X 5-inch loaf pan with foil. Press in the beef mixture. In a separate bowl, combine the topping ingredients, mixing well. Spread topping over the meat loaf.

Bake at 400° for 35 to 45 minutes or until done. Drain off fat. Rest meat loaf 5 minutes before serving.

SUMMER MEAT LOAF

½ c. chopped onion

½ c. shredded carrot

½ c. chopped green pepper

2 slightly beaten eggs

1 ½ c. soft breadcrumbs

1 c. cottage cheese

1 tsp. salt

1 tsp. poultry seasoning

2 lb. ground beef

¾ c. catsup

Cook onion, carrot, and pepper, covered, in a small amount of boiling water for 5 minutes; drain. Mix eggs, crumbs, cheese, salt, and poultry seasoning. Drain. Stir in vegetables. Add beef; mix well.

Pat into 9 x 5 x 3-inch loaf pan. Bake, uncovered, in a 350° oven about 1 ½ hours. Drain meat loaf. Serves 8.

MINI MEAT LOAVES AND VEGETABLES

1 ½ lb, lean ground beef

½ tsp. salt

1 egg

1 (8 oz) can tomato sauce

½ tsp. Italian seasoning

1 (2.8 oz.) can /French fried
   Onions

6 small redskin potatoes, sliced
thin

1 (16 oz.) bag frozen broccoli.
corn, red pepper combination,
thawed and drained

Combine meat, salt, gg, ½ can tomato sauce, Italian seasoning and ½ can onions. In 9 x 13-inch baking dish, form 3 mini loaves. Place potatoes around loaves. Bake, covered, at 375° for 35 minutes.

Place vegetables around loaves; stir to combine with the potatoes. Lightly season with salt and pepper, if desired. Top meat loaves with remaining tomato sauce.

Bake, uncovered, 15 minutes. Top loaves with remaining onions. Bake, uncovered, 5 minutes longer. Makes 3 to 6 servings.

BAKED CHICKEN BREASTS SUPREME

1 ½ c. plain yogurt or sour cream

¼ c. lemon juice

½ tsp. Worcestershire sauce

½ tsp. celery seed

½ tsp. paprika

1 garlic clove, minced

½ tsp. salt

¼ tsp. pepper

8 boneless, skinless chicken
breasts

2 c. fine dry breadcrumbs

In large bowl, combine first eight ingredients. Place chicken in mixture and turn to coat. Cover and marinate overnight in refrigerator.

Remove chicken from marinade, Coat each piece with crumbs. Arrange on a shallow baking pan. Bake, uncovered, at 350° for 45 minutes or until juices run clear.

BATTER FRIED CHICKEN

1 medium fryer, cut in pieces

1 egg, slightly beaten

1 c. milk

1 c. flour

Combine egg and milk. Sprinkle chicken with salt and pepper. Dip chicken in flour. Then egg mixture, then flour. Fry in hot oil until golden brown.

COUNTRY FRIED CHICKEN

1 (3 LB.) fryer chicken

¾ to 1 c. buttermilk

cooking oil (for frying)

Coating:

2 c. flour

1 ½ tsp. salt

½ tsp. pepper

½ tsp. garlic powder

½ tsp. onion powder

1 Tbsp, paprika

¼ tsp. ground sage

¼ tsp. ground thyme

1/8 tsp. baking powder

Wash and pat dry chicken pieces with paper towel. Place in a large, flat dish. Pour buttermilk over chicken. Cover and allow to soak at least 1 hour or overnight in refrigerator.

Combine coating ingredients in double-strength paper bag and shake chicken pieces, one at a time, to coat well. Lay coated pieces on wax paper for 15 minutes to allow coating to dry.

Meanwhile, pour oil to 1/2-inch depth in electric skillet and heat to 350°. Fry chicken, several pieces at a time, for about 3 minutes on each side. Do not overcrowd. Reduce heat to 325°. Cook chicken for 25 to 30 minutes, turning occasionally. Remove to paper towel-lined platter.

OLD-FASHIONED CHICKEN AND DUMPLINGS

3 lb. fryer, cut in pieces

2 chicken bouillon cubes

2 c. all-purpose flour

½ tsp. salt

4 tsp. baking powder

2/3 c. milk

2 tsp. melted butter

1 egg, well beaten

Place chicken pieces and bouillon in large pot. Add 2 cups water. Cover and cook over Medium heat until tender.

Sift together flour, salt, and baking powder. Add milk, butter, and egg. Mix thoroughly and add more milk and flour as needs to make a soft dough.

Turn onto floured board and knead until smooth. Divide dough into four parts and roll each very thin. Cut into 2-inch squares. Slide onto a piece of wax paper until all are cut.

Remove lid from chicken. Carefully slide a few dumplings into pot. Submerge each with fork around chicken. When all squares are in, cover, lower heat and cook 15 minutes without lifting lid. Makes 6 to 8 servings.

CURRIED COUNTRY CHICKEN

3 lb. frying chicken, cut up
1 tsp. salt
¼ tsp. pepper
2 Tbsp. oil
1 medium onion, sliced
¾ c. chopped green pepper

1 garlic clove, minced
½ c. raisins
¼ tsp. curry powder
½ tsp. thyme leaves
16 oz. can whole tomatoes,
  cut up

Sprinkle chicken pieces with salt and pepper. In large skillet, brown chicken in oil. Remove Chicken from skillet.

In same skillet, sauté onion, green pepper and garlic just until crisp and tender. Add raisins, curry, thyme, tomatoes, and browned chicken. Cover, simmer 30 to 40 minutes or until chicken is tender. Serve over rice.

SWEET AND SOUR CHICKEN WINGS

1 lb. chicken wings

Sauce:

¾ c. Sugar
½ c. Chicken stock
½ c. catsup

1 Tbsp. soy sauce
¼ tsp. salt

Make stock from tips of wings and water. Fry chicken as usual. Combine remaining ingredients and bring to boil. Stir until dissolved and ingredients are blended; pour over wings. Bake, covered, at 350° for 15 minutes.

SOUTH SEAS CHICKEN AND BANANAS

¼ c. lemon juice

1 (14 oz.) can sweetened

Condensed milk

1/3 c. milk

½ c. flaked coconut

1/8 tsp. ground cardamom

6 very firm bananas, halved

lengthwise

3 c. cornflake crumbs

5 to 6 lb. chicken pieces

¾ c. butter or margarine, melted

In a food processor or blender, blend the lemon juice, condensed milk, milk, coconut, and cardamom until smooth. Pour into a bowl. Dip bananas into milk mixture; roll in cornflakes and set aside.

Dip chicken into remaining milk mixture. Roll in the remaining cornflakes. Place in two greased 13 x 9 x 2-inch baking pans. Drizzle with ½ cup of the melted butter.

Bake, uncovered, at 350° for 1 hour. Arrange bananas over the chicken. Drizzle with remaining butter. Bake 15 minutes longer or until chicken juices run clear.

BUTTERMILK FRIED CHICKEN

1 broiler-fryer chicken (2 ½ to 3

Lb.), cut up

1 c. buttermilk

1 c. all-purpose flour

1 ½ tsp. salt

½ tsp. pepper

cooking oil (for frying)

Place chicken pieces in a large, flat dish. Pour buttermilk over. Cover and refrigerate for 1 hour.

Combine flour, salt, and pepper in a double-strength paper bag. Drain chicken pieces. Toss, one at a time, in flour mixture. Shake off excess. Place on waxed paper for 15 minutes to dry.

Heat ¼ inch of oil in large skillet. Fry chicken until browned on all sides.

CHICKEN-CORNMEAL CASSEROLE

1 (10 ¾ oz.) can condensed
Cream of chicken soup
2 c. cooked, cubed chicken
1 (1o oz.) pkg. frozen peas
¼ c. sliced water chestnuts
2 tsp. minced, dried onion

2/3 c. packaged biscuit mix
1/3 c. cornmeal
½ tsp. dried basil, crushed
1/3 c. milk
1 beaten egg

In saucepan, combine cream of chicken soup, chicken, frozen peas, water chestnuts and dried onion. Heat until bubbly, stirring occasionally.

In bowl, combine the packaged biscuit mix, cornmeal, and basil. 'Stir in milk and egg just until moistened.

Turn chicken mixture inti a 1 ½-quart casserole. Pour biscuit mixture overall, spreading evenly to edge of casserole.

Bake in a 375° oven about 20 minutes or until biscuit topper is done. Makes 4 servings.

CORNBREAD DRESSING

½ c. butter or margarine
5 or 6 c. cornbread, crumbled
1 ½ qt. (6 c.) soft breadcrumbs
¼ c. cooking oil
1 c. diced celery
½ c. chopped onion

1 ½ c. broth from giblets
2 tsp. salt
½ tsp. pepper
1 1.2 tsp. poultry seasoning
2 beaten eggs
½ c. chopped green pepper

Cut butter into very small pieces and mix with cornbread and breadcrumbs.

Heat oil in a heavy skillet. Add celery, onion and green pepper and sauté slowly for 5 minutes. Add to cornbread mixture. Add seasonings, mixing thoroughly. Add well-beaten eggs. Sprinkle cooled broth over surface, stirring lightly, until dressing is of desired moistness.

Stuff lightly into breast region and body cavity of the bird. Makes enough for 12-pound turkey. Cook turkey according to directions.

CRISP CRUSTED BAKED CHICKEN

1 frying chicken (3 to 3 ¼ lb.),
Out up
1 egg
2 Tbsp. milk
1 c. instant potato flakes

1 tsp. garlic powder
¼ c. grated Parmesan cheese
¼ c. butter or margarine
celery leaves and thinly sliced
celery (for garnish)

Wash chicken pieces and pat dry; set aside. Beat egg and milk in bowl. In another bowl, mix potato flakes, garlic powder and Parmesan cheese. Roll chicken first in egg mix, then in the potato flakes mixture.

Melt butter in shallow baking pan. Roll coated chicken pieces in the butter and place them, skin side up, in the pan. Bake at 400° for 45 to 50 minutes or until juices from thighs run clear when pierced with a fork.

Transfer to serving platter. Garnish with celery leaves and celery slices and serve.

MOCK CHICKEN LEGS

1 lb. lean pork
1 lb. boneless veal
1 ½ tsp. salt
Pepper to taste
1 egg, beaten

¼ c. milk
½ c. fine, dry breadcrumbs
¼ c. shortening
½ c. meat stock or water

Trim off excess fat from pork and cut both kinds of meat into 1 ½-inch cubes. Stick skewers through the center of these cubes, alternating pork and veal and using enough the center of these cubes, alternating pork and veal and using enough to fill skewers a little more than half full. Sprinkle salt and pepper over meat then press into shape.

Dip in egg diluted with milk, then roll in crumbs until well coated. Brown slowly on all sides in the hot shortening in a heavy skillet. Add the stock. Reduce heat, cover and simmer slowly over low heat about 1 hour or until very tender.

Make gravy from drippings, if desired, to serve with legs. Makes 5 to 6 servings.

CHEESE- STUFFED TROUT

½ c. sliced mushrooms

½ c. thinly sliced green onions

2 Tsp. Grated Parmesan cheese

4 dressed trout (about ½ lb. each)

salt and pepper

In small bowl, combine mushrooms, onions and cheese. Spoon evenly into cavity of each fish. Season with salt and pepper. Season with salt and pepper. Securely close cavities with toothpicks or skewers to keep stuffing inside.

When ready to barbecue, place fish on greased grill 3 to 4 inches from hot coals. Cook 15 to 20 minutes, turning once, until fish flaked. Makes 4 servings.

FRIED FISH

½ c. fine white cornmeal

½ c. all-purpose flour

1 tsp. salt

1 tsp. grated lemon peel

1 tsp. garlic powder

½ tsp. cayenne pepper

½ tsp. black pepper

2 lb. whiting fillets

1 c. peanut oil

Combine cornmeal, flour, salt, lemon peel, garlic powder, cayenne pepper and black pepper in large bowl. Dredge fish fillets in cornmeal mixture to coat all sides.

Heat oil in heavy, deep skillet. Add a few fish fillets to hot oil without crowding pan. Brown on both sides 5 or 6 minutes. Remove fish to paper toweling to drain. Repeat to cook all fish.

SMOKED FISH

1 lb. smoked fish (4 medium)

1/2 c. water

2 Tbsp. lemon juice

1/8 tsp. sugar

½ tsp. salt

dash of pepper

1 Tbsp. butter

2 Tbsp. chopped parsley

Place clean, rinsed fish in a skillet. Add next 5 ingredients. Cover and cook over medium heat for 10 minutes or until fish are heated through and the liquid has evaporated.

Place hot fillets on a platter. Drizzle with melted butter and sprinkle with parsley.

SHRIMP LOUIS

6 c. water
2 lb. unpeeled, medium size,
Fresh shrimp
½ c. mayonnaise
2 Tbsp. chopped green onions
2 Tbsp. chopped green pepper
1 large, hard-cooked egg, finely
  Chopped

1 Tbsp. chopped pimiento
½ tsp. lemon juice
½ tsp. salt
½ tsp. pepper
curly leaf lettuce
shredded iceberg lettuce

Bring water to a boil. Add shrimp and cook 3 to 5 minutes or until shrimp turn pink. Drain well. Rinse with cold water. Chill. Peel and devein shrimp. Cover and chill thoroughly.

Combine mayonnaise and next 7 ingredients; stir well. Pour mayonnaise mixture over shrimp and toss gently.

Line a shell-shaped bowl or salad bowl with leaf lettuce. Top with shredded iceberg lettuce. Spoon shrimp mixture evenly over shredded lettuce. Makes 6 servings

SHRIMP SCAMPI

2 lb. unpeeled, jumbo, fresh
Shrimp
1 medium onion, finely chopped
4 cloves garlic, minced
1/2 c. butter or margarine, melted
2 Tbsp. lemon juice

½ tsp. dried tarragon
½ tsp. steak sauce
½ tsp. Worcestershire sauce
¼ tsp. hot sauce
hot, cooked fettuccine
2 Tbsp. chopped fresh parsley

Peel and devein shrimp. Cook onion and garlic a butter in a large skillet over medium. Heat, stirring constantly, 4 minutes. Add lemon juice and next 4 ingredients. Bring to a boil. Add shrimp and cook, stirring constantly, 3 to 5 minutes or until shrimp turn pink. Serve over fettuccine. Sprinkle with parsley. Serves 4 to 6.

FILE GUMBO

½ c. butter
2 Tbsp. flour
½ c. chopped onion
2 qt. hot water
8 crab legs, cleaned
1 lb. shelled, deveined shrimp

2 slices raw ham, chopped
1 medium Polish sausage, sliced
1 medium chicken, cut in pieces
2 garlic cloves, chopped
salt and cayenne pepper to taste
2 Tbsp. file powder

Blend butter and flour in skillet over low heat. Stir constantly until brown and the color of peanut butter. Stir in chopped onion, sauté slightly.

Pour mixture into large pot. Mix in 2 quarts hot water. Add remaining ingredients, except file powder. Bring mixture to a boil. Simmer gently for one hour. In the last 5 minutes of cooking, add file powder. Do not boil again.

Note: Brown chicken, sausage, and shrimp in separate pan before adding to mixture.

OLD-FASHIONED BAKED HAM

1 (8 oz.) can pineapple slices
1 canned ham (5 lb.)
½ c. packed brown sugar
¼ tsp. ground cloves

1 tsp. dry mustard
1 Tbsp. vinegar
maraschino cherries

Drain pineapple, reserving 2 tablespoons juice; set aside. Place ham in a baking pan. Bake at 350° for 30 minutes.

Combine brown sugar, cloves, mustard, and vinegar in a small bowl; stir in reserved pineapple juice. Score ham. Place pineapple slices and cherries on top of ham; spoon glaze over fruit and ham. Bake for another 40 to 45 minutes, basting occasionally.

HAM SKILLET DINNER

6 oz. (3 c.) uncooked medium egg noodles
2 c. cubed, cooked ham
1 Tbsp. Instant minced onion
1 ½ c. milk

1 tsp. Worcestershire sauce
1 (15 oz.) can Green Giant cream-style corn
1 c. cubed American cheese

In large skillet, combine all ingredients, except cheese; mix well. Bring to a boil. Cover. Simmer 18 to 20 minutes or until noodles are tender, stirring occasionally. Stir in cheese. Cook until cheese begins to melt. Serve immediately.

HAM AND SWEET POTATO CASSEROLE

1 ½ c. diced, cooked ham
1 Tbsp. butter or ham fat
6 c. hot, mashed sweet potatoes (1 2/2 LB.)

1 ½ tbsp. Lemon juice
2 eggs, beaten
½ c. milk
½ tsp. salt or to taste

Brown ham slightly in butter or ham fat. Whip potatoes until smooth and combine with beaten eggs, milk, lemon juice and salt, whip again thoroughly. Mix with the browned ham and drippings.

Turn into an 8-cup greased casserole. Bake, uncovered, in a moderate oven (350°) for 45 minutes. Serve hot. Makes 5 servings.

TASTY PORK CHOPS

4 pork chops (1/2 to 3/4inch thick)
1 Tbsp. oil

1 clove garlic, minced

Sauce:

2 tsp. Oil
4 Tbsp. broth
4 Tbsp. soy sauce
2 Tbsp. brown sugar

¼ tsp. crushed red pepper
2 tsp. Cornstarch
2 Tbsp. water

Heat oil in skillet. Brown chops on both sides. Remove and add a little more oil, if needed. Sauté garlic for a minute, being careful not to burn it.

Combine oil, broth, soy sauce, brown sugar, and red pepper. Place chops in skillet. Pour sauce over them. Cover tightly, Simmer over low heat until chops are tender and cooled through,30 to 35 minutes. Add little water, if needed, to keep sauce from cooking down too much. Turn once. Remove chops to platter.

Stir in cornstarch dissolved in water. Cool until thickened. Pour over chops and serve with noodles or spaghetti.

BISCUIT STUFFING ON CHOPS

6 PORK CHOPS (1/2 INCH THICK)
1 Tbsp. oil
10 ¾ oz. condensed cream`
Of chicken soup
1 c. chopped celery
1 c. chopped onions

1 egg
¼ tsp. pepper
1/8 tsp. poultry seasoning or sage
7.5 oz. Can Pillsbury refrigerated
biscuits

Heat oven to 350°. In large skillet, brown pork chops in oil. Place in ungreased 13 x 9-inch pan.

In medium bowl, combine soup celery, onions, egg, pepper, and poultry seasoning; mix well. Separate dough into 10 biscuits; cut each biscuit into 6 pieces. Stir biscuit pieces into soup mixture, spoon over meat.

Bake at 350° for 45 to 50 minutes or until biscuit pieces are golden brown. Makes 6 servings.

SAVORY SWISS STEAK

2 LB. round steak
½ c. flour
1 small onion
½ c. water

¼ c. shortening
2 tsp. salt
1 (8 oz.) can stewed tomatoes
¼ tsp. pepper

Rinse steak and cut into serving pieces. Sprinkle on both sides with salt and pepper. Dip into flour. Melt shortening in a heavy skillet and brown the steak slowly on both sides. Add onion and sauté. Drain off fat. Return meat to skillet; add tomatoes and water.

Cover and simmer for about 1 ½ hours or until very tender. Add more water, if needed, during cooking to prevent from going dry.

SLOW-COOKED PEPPER STEAK

2 lb. beef round steak
2 Tbsp. cooking oil
¼ c. soy sauce
1 c. chopped onion
1 garlic clove, minced
1 tsp. sugar
½ tsp. salt
¼ tsp. pepper

¼ tsp. ginger
4 tomatoes, cubed or 1 (16 oz.)
can tomato with liquid
2 large green peppers, cut into
strips
½ c. cold water
1 Tbsp. cornstarch
cooked noodles or rice

Cut beef into 3 x 1-inch strips: brown in oil in a skillet. Transfer to a slow cooker. Combine the next seven ingredients; pour over beef. Cover and cook on low for 5 to 6 hours or until meat is tender. Add tomatoes and green peppers. Cook on low for 1 hour longer.

Combine the cold water and cornstarch to make a paste. Stir into liquid in slow cooker and cook on high until thickened. Serve over noodles or rice.

SAVORY BEEF STEW

2 lb. beef stew meat
4 slices bacon, cut into 1-inch
Pieces
1 (18 oz.) jar brown gravy
1 (14.5 oz) can diced, peeled
Tomatoes, undrained
1 tsp. dried thyme leaves

½ tsp. salt
¼ tsp. pepper
1 lb. baby carrots
8 new red potatoes, quartered
2 small onions, cut into eighths
1 (8 oz.) pkg. fresh, whole
mushrooms

In medium skillet, over medium-high heat, cook beef and bacon until beef is browned; drain.

In 4-quart crock-pot, combine gravy, tomatoes, thyme, salt, and pepper. Add beef, bacon, and remaining ingredients; stir gently to combine. Cover. Cook on low setting for 8 to 10 hours or until meat and vegetables are tender.

BARBECUED SPARERIBS NO. 1

3 lb. spareribs
1 medium onion, chopped
1 Tbsp. butter
1 Tbsp. vinegar
1 Tbsp. sugar
3 Tbsp. lemon juice

2 Tbsp. Worcestershire sauce
½ Tbsp. prepared mustard
½ c. water
½ c. chopped celery
2 tsp. salt
dash of cayenne

Wipe spareribs with damp cloth; cut in serving size pieces. Place in a shallow baking pan and bake, uncovered, in a moderate oven (350°) for 30 minutes.

Meanwhile, sauté onion in butter for 5 minutes, then add remaining ingredients, mix well. Simmer 5 minutes. Pour over the spareribs and continue for an hour longer, basting from time to time with the sauce in the bottom of the pan.

BARBECUED SPARERIBS NO. 2

3 lb. spareribs
1 ½ tsp. salt
¼ tsp. pepper
¼ tsp. paprika
¼ tsp. chili powder

¼ tsp. poultry seasoning
1 small onion
1 (8 oz.) can tomato sauce
1 ½ c. water
1 tsp. sugar

Place ribs in large, shallow baking pan so that they are in a single layer, if possible. For easier handling, measure seasonings and spices and mix together. Sprinkle generously over ribs on both sides. Slice onion over top and pour tomato sauce overall. Add water and sprinkle sugar over sauce.

Bake in a moderate over (325°) from 2 to 2 ½ hours or until very tender. Baste often and turn ribs several times during cooking. Add more water, if necessary, but sauce should be thick enough to cling to meat when done.

BARBECUED SHORT RIBS

6 lb. lean beef short ribs
1 tsp. salt

½ tsp. ground pepper
1 recipe Texas Barbecue Sauce

Brown ribs slowly in their own fat in a large skillet. Pour off drippings. Sprinkle ribs with salt and pepper. Cover tightly. Cook over low heat, turning often, 1 ½ to 2 hours. Arrange ribs on rack in broiler pan.

Skim and discard fat from juices in pan. Add juices to barbecue sauce. Brush ribs with sauce. Broil, brushing and turning ribs often, until well glazed, about 30 minutes. Heat remaining sauce and serve with ribs.

SHORT RIBS POT ROAST

2 lb. beef short ribs
¼ c. flour
2 Tbsp. shortening
2 tsp. salt

1/8 tsp. pepper
1 small onion, sliced
¼ c. water

Cut ribs into individual servings and dredge in flour. Brown slowly on all sides in the hated shortening in a heavy., iron skillet, allowing 20 to 30 minutes for browning. Add seasonings, onion, and water.

Cover tightly and simmer gently for 2 hours or until meat is tender. More water may be added, if needed, to prevent pan from going dry.

CRANBERRY PORK ROAST

1 boneless rolled pork loin roast
(3 lb.)
1 (16 oz.) can jellied cranberry
Sauce
½ c. sugar
½ c. cranberry juice

1 tsp. dry mustard
¼ tsp. ground cloves
2 Tbsp. cornstarch
2 Tbsp. cold water
salt to taste

Place pork roast in a slow cooker. In a medium bowl., mash cranberry sauce. Stir in sugar, cranberry juice, mustard, and cloves. Pour over roast. Cover and cook on low for 6 to 8 hours or until meat is tender. Remove roast and keep warm.

Skim fat from juices. Measure 2 cups, adding water if necessary, and pour into a saucepan. Bring to a boil over medium-high heat. Combine the cornstarch and cold water to make a paste; stir into gravy. Cook and stir until thickened. Season with salt. Serve with sliced pork.

SALMON CROQUETTES

1 lb. pink salmon, undrained
2 eggs, slightly beaten
½ c. seasoned mashed potatoes
½ c. crunchy wheat germ
Salt and pepper to taste

1 Tbsp. lemon juice
¼ tap. Garlic powder
Parmesan cheese
½ c. flour
½ c. shortening

Drain salmon, mash fine. Stir in eggs and potatoes, blending well. Add wheat germ, seasonings, and lemon juice, mixing thoroughly. Divide into ¼-cup portions and shape into flat patties, about ½ inch thick. Mix Parmesan cheese with flour.

Heat shortening in heavy skillet. Lightly roll patties in flour mixture. Lay patties in skillet and brown on both sides to a rich, golden color. Remove to a hot platter and garnish with parsley and lemon wedges, if desired.

ROAST TURKEY

3 tsp. salt
2 tsp. pepper

½ c. butter

Rinse turkey inside and out with cold water and drain thoroughly. Place in roaster large enough to hold a 12-pound bird. Mix salt and pepper together and sprinkle half inside of the turkey; rub the other half on the outside. Stuff with cornbread dressing.

Cut butter in small pieces and dot randomly on bird. Cover with roaster lid and bake according to weight of bird.

MEXICAN CORN SCRAMBLE

1 large, chopped onion
¼ c. butter
10 eggs, beaten
12 oz. can Green Giant Mexicorn
(Kernel com with sweet
Peppers)

2 ½ oz. can sliced ripe olives,
drained
1 c. shredded Monterey Jack
cheese
1 c. sliced dry salami or wieners
tortilla chips
Taco sauce

In large skillet, cook onion in margarine over medium heat until crisp and tender. Add eggs, corn and olives. Stir gently until eggs begin to cook. Add cheese and salami; stir until blended. Continue cooking until eggs are set and cheese is melted.

Stand tortilla chips around edge of skillet. Top with taco sauce. To eat, serve hot, scooped up onto chips or with a fork with chips as an accompaniment. Makes 8 servings.

LIVER RIBBONS

1 lb. calves' liver
1 large onion, sliced
½ tsp. salt

2 Tbsp. wheat germ
4 Tbsp. oil
½ tsp. pepper

Rinse liver and cut into strips. Pour oil into skillet. When hot, sauté onion. Salt and pepper liver and coat with wheat germ.

Sauté in skillet with onion 5 minutes on both sides. Add ¼ cup water. Cover and simmer for 5 minutes. Serve immediately.

PINEAPPLE SAUSAGE STIR-FRY

2 medium carrots, cut into 1-inch
long julienne strips
1 (8 oz.) can pineapple chunks
¼ c. unsweetened pineapple
Juice
1 (6 oz.) pkg. frozen pea pods
3 Tbsp. teriyaki sauce

4 tsp. cornstarch
1 Tbsp. brown sugar
1 (12 oz.) pkg. fully cooked
smoked sausage links, cut
crosswise into thirds
chow Mein noodles

Cook carrots in a small amount of boiling, salted water for 7 to 10 minutes or until tender. Drain pineapple chunks, reserving juice; set pineapple aside. Combine the reserved pineapple juice to make 1 14 cups liquid. Run hot water over frozen pea pods in a colander until thawed; set aside. In small bowl, stir in pineapple juice mixture.

In wok or large skillet, stir-fry sausage for about 5 minutes or until brown. Stir the teriyaki mixture. Stir into wok or skillet. Cook and stir until mixture is thickened and bubbly. Stir in carrots, pineapple chunks and pea pods. Cover and cook 2 minutes more. Serve at once over chow Mein noodles. Makes 4 servings.

AMAZING QUICHE

2 ¼ Cc. milk
5 eggs
½ c. all-purpose flour
2 tsp. minced, dried onion

1/4 tap. Dried marjoram, crushed
1 c. (4 oz.) shredded Brick or
Monterey Jack cheese
½ c. grated Parmesan cheese

Grease a 10-inch pie plate or quiche pan. In a blender container, combine milk, eggs, flour, onion, marjoram and ¼ teaspoon salt. Cover. Blend 15 seconds. Pour into pie plate. Top with cheeses.

Bake in a 400° oven for 20 to 25 minutes or until a knife inserted near center comes out clean. Let stand 5 minutes. Serves 6.

Vegetables

How To Can Vegetables

POINTS ON PACKING

Raw pack, Pack cold raw vegetables (except corn, lima beans, and peas) lightly into container and cover with boiling water.

Hot pack. Preheat vegetables in water or steam. Cover with cooking liquid or boiling water. Cooking liquid is recommended for packing most vegetables because it may contain minerals and vitamins dissolved out of the food. Boiling water is recommended when cooking liquid is dark, gritty, or strong-flavored, and when there isn't enough cooking liquid.

HOW TO CHECK CANNING JARS

The first step in home canning should take place long before food and equipment are assembled and ready to go. Jars and other supplies should be checked prior to the canning session. In that way, you can replace damaged supplies and purchase new ones to avoid costly delays or inconvenience. Here are some tips to help you.

Choosing mason Jars. Jars manufactured especially for home canning generically are called maso jars and must be used when preserving. They ae designed with a specially threaded mouth for proper sealing with mason lids. So, can with standard mason jars only.

Preparing glass jars, Check all jars, rings, and lids carefully. Discard any with nicks or crack in top sealing edge and threads that may prevent airtight seals. Rings should be free of dents or rust. Select the size of closures—wide mouth or regular—that fits your jar. Wash jars in hot, soapy water and rinse well. Then place in boiling water for 10-15 minutes. Keep jars in hot water until ready to use. Boil lid according to package directions.

Closing glass jars. Always wipe jar rim clean after food product is packed. Place lid on jar with button side up. Screw rings on firmly, but don't force. Do not re-tighten rings after processing or cooling.

A new lid that snaps down and clicks as the jar cools, providing visible proof of sealing, called Magic Button® is made by Owens-Illinois. Its red button pops up when the seal is broken. The Magic Mason jars that go with the special lids have metric measurements as well as customary U.S. measurements molded on the side.

Jar transfer. Use jar lifter or long handled canning longs to transfer jars to and from canner safely. Place hot jars on rack or towel, allowing 2-inches of air space on all sides for jars to cool evenly.

PROCESSING IN A PRESSURE CANNER

Use a steam-pressure canner for processing all vegetables except tomatoes and pickled vegetables. Direction. Follow the manufacturer's directions for the canner you are using. Here are a few pointers on the use of any steam-pressure canner:

- Put 2 or 3 inches of boiling water in the bottom of the canner; the amount of water to use depends on the size and shape of the canner.
- Set filled glass jars or tin cans on rack in canner so that steam can flow around each container. If two layers of cans or jars are put in, stagger the second layer. Use a rack between layers of glass jars.
- Fasten canner cover securely so that no steam can escape except through vent (petcock or weighted gage opening)
- Watch until steam pours steadily from vent. Let it escape for 10 minutes or more to drive all air from the canner. Then close petcock or put on weighted gage.
- Let pressure rise to 10 pounds (240 degrees F.) The moment this pressure is reached, start counting processing time. Keep pressure constant by regulating heat under the canner. Do not lower pressure by opening petcock. Keep drafts from blowing on canner.
- When processing time is up, remove canner from heat immediately.

With Glass Jars, let canner stand until the pressure is zero. Never try to rush the cooling by pouring cold water over the canner. When pressure registers zero, wait a minute or two, then slowly open petcock or take off weighted gage. Unfasten cover and tilt the jar side up so steam escapes away from you. Take jars from canner.

❑ VEGETABLES

CANDIED SWEET POTATOES

5 medium sweet potatoes
½ c. water
½ c. brown sugar
½ tsp. nutmeg
2 Tbsp. butter

½ c. granulated sugar
¼ tsp. salt
½ tsp. cinnamon
½ tsp. vanilla

Wash potatoes and cook, covered, in large pot until tender, about 45 minutes. Cool and peel. Slice lengthwise and place half the potatoes in 13 x 9 x 2-inch casserole.

Mix together sugars, salt and spices. Sprinkle half of the mixture over potatoes. Add the second layer of potatoes and sprinkle remaining mixture over potatoes. Mix vanilla with water; pour overall. Dot with the butter. Cover and bake in 375° oven for 30 minutes.

CANDIED YAMS

6 medium yams
½ c. molasses
½ c. brown sugar, packed
½ c. milk

½ c. butter or margarine
¼ tsp. cloves
¼ tsp. cinnamon
¼ tsp. nutmeg

Boll and peel yams. Cut into quarters lengthwise. Place in shallow, buttered pan. Pour molasses over yams and dot with butter. Sprinkle brown sugar and spices over yams. Pour milk overall and bake at 350° for 30 minutes. Slices of pineapple may be added on top before baking.

CORN PUDDING

4 eggs, whipped
1 ¾ c. milk
1 stick (1/2 c.) melted butter
1 (16 oz.) can corn

1 (16 oz.) bag frozen corn,
slightly thawed
black pepper to taste
2 tsp. salt
2 Tbsp. sugar

Blend in mixer, eggs, milk, and melted butter. Add remaining ingredients. Pour into greased 9 x 13-inch baking dish. Bake at 325° for 1 ½ hours or until golden brown on top and edges.

FRIED CORN

½ c. butter
5 c. corn, cut off cob

¾ tsp. salt
½ tsp. pepper

Heat butter sizzling hot in skillet. Add corn and enough water to give consistency of thin gravy. Season with salt and cook, with constant stirring, for 5 minutes. Then reduce heat to simmering. Cover tightly and cook about 20 minutes, stirring occasionally.

The corn, at this point, should be quite thick. Good served hot or cold.

STUFFED CABBAGE

1 lb. ground beef
1 small onion, chopped
1 egg
¾ c. cooked rice
¼ tsp. pepper
½ tsp. salt

¼ c. dark corn syrup
½ c. raisins
2 Tbsp. sugar
2 Tbsp. vinegar
1 ½ c. gingersnap crumbs
1 (26 oz.) can tomatoes

In large bowl, combine beef, onion, egg, rice salt and pepper. Mix with hands until well blended. Set aside. Cook cabbage leaves about 5 minutes in boiling, salted water. Remove and drain on paper towels.

Place about ¼ cup of beef mixture on each cabbage leaf and roll up, egg roll style. Fasten with toothpick. Place rolls, toothpick down, in baking pan, packed tightly together to keep their shape.

In large bowl, combine tomatoes and juice, corn syrup, raisins, sugar, and vinegar; mix well. Pour evenly over cabbage rolls.

Cover pan loosely with foil and bake at 350° for one hour. Remove foil and sprinkle gingersnap crumbs over top of cabbage rolls. Re-cover and simmer or bake an additional 30 minutes. Serves 6.

POTATOES SUPREME

1 (2 lb.) bag frozen hash browns, Thawed
2. sour cream

2 c. grated Cheddar cheese
1 can cream of chicken soup
½ c. melted butter or margarine

Mix all ingredients together and spread in a 9 x 13-inch baking dish. Bake at 350° for 15 minutes, then stir thoroughly. Continue baking for about 1 hour, until bubbly and lightly browned. Extra cheese may be sprinkled on top, if desired.

FRIED GREEN TOMATOES

3 medium green tomatoes

3 ripe tomatoes

½ c. flour

¾ tsp. salt

¼ tsp. pepper

½ c. shortening

Wash tomatoes. Remove stems and cut into half-inch, crosswise slices. Mix flour, salt and pepper and dip both sides of tomato slices into the mixture.

Heat shortening in skillet until sizzling hot. Put in the tomatoes and cook rather quickly until browned on underside. Then turn tomatoes carefully. Reduce heat and cook until thoroughly hot and soft through center. Remove to a hot platter and serve piping hot, either plain or with a cheese sauce.

OLD-FASHIONED BAKED BEANS

2 lb. dried navy beans

2 qt. cold water

1 medium onion, sliced

1 tsp. salt

4 tsp. cider vinegar

1 tsp. prepared mustard

2 Tbsp. brown sugar

½ c. molasses

½ c. ketchup

1/8 tsp. black pepper

½ lb. salt pork, sliced

Wash beans thoroughly. Add cold water, cover. Heat to boiling and simmer for 30 minutes. Drain, but do not discard, the liquid.

Place onion slices in bottom of a ten-quart casserole. Combine the next 7 ingredients and turn into the casserole. And the beans and enough hot, drained liquid or water to cover, about 2 ½ cups. Arrange salt pork slices on top.

Cover and bake in very slow oven (250°) 7 to 8 hours. After 4 hours, stir and add more water, if needed. Beans should be just covered with thick, luscious liquid. Remove cover 1 hour before end of cooking time to allow salt pork to brown. Makes 10 to 12 servings.

BLACK-EYED PEAS

1 lb. (2 c.) black-eyed peas

8 c. cold water

1 ham hock

½ tsp. red pepper flakes

salt and pepper to taste

Wash beans thoroughly and turn into a 4-qart saucepan. Add the cold water and ham hock. Heat to boiling and simmer until bens and ham hock are very tender, about 3 hours.

About 15 minutes before they are done, add red pepper. Season to suit taste.

BROCCOLI RICE CASSEROLE

1 small onion, chopped
½ c. chopped celery
1 (1o oz.) pkg. frozen, chopped
Broccoli, thawed
1 Tbsp. butter or margarine

1 (8 oz.) jar process cheese
spread
1 (10 ¾ oz.) can condensed
cream of mushroom soup
1 (5 oz.) can evaporated milk
3 c. cooked rice

In large skillet, over medium heat, sauté onion, celery, and broccoli in butter for 3 to 5 minutes. Stir in cheese, soup and milk until smooth.

Place rice in a greased 8-inch square baking dish. Pour cheese mixture over; do not stir. Bake, uncovered, at 325° for 25 to 30 minutes or until hot and bubbly.

PINEAPPLE RICE

3 Tbsp. butter or margarine
3 Tbsp. sesame oil
1 c. chopped onion
4 (14 ½ oz.) cans chicken broth
3 c. uncooked brown rice
1 tsp. salt

½ tsp. black pepper
1 (15 ¼ oz.) can pineapple
tidbits, drained
¼ c. finely chopped green pepper
¼ c. finely chopped sweet red
pepper

In Dutch oven over medium heat, combine butter and oil. Add onion and cook until tender. Add broth, rice, salt, and pepper. Bring to a boil. Reduce heat. Cover and simmer 50 to 60 minutes or until all liquid is absorbed. Stir in remaining ingredients; cook 2 minutes longer.

GREEN BEANS AND NEW POTATOES

2 lb. fresh green beans
2 lb. unpeeled new potatoes,
Quartered
10 slices bacon
1 onion, chopped
2 cloves garlic, minced

½ c. chopped fresh parsley
¼ c. apple cider vinegar
2 tsp. dried oregano leaves
1 tsp. salt
½ tsp. black pepper

Wash beans: trim ends and remove strings. Cut into 1 ½-inch pieces. In a Dutch oven, combine green beans and potatoes. Cover with salted water and bring to a boil. Cover and cook until potatoes are tender. Drain in a colander.

In large skillet, cook bacon until crisp. Drain on paper towels, crumble. Add onion and garlic to bacon drippings. Cook until onion is tender. Stir in green beans and potatoes, parsley, vinegar, oregano, salt and pepper. Stirring occasionally, cook until edges of potatoes begin to brown. Stir in crumbled bacon.

MUSTARD GREENS

2 lb. mustard greens
6 c. boiling water
3 strips bacon

1 ½ tsp, salt
½ tsp. sugar
¼ tsp. red pepper

Wash greens in warm water. Chop in small pieces. Place in large pot. Cover with boiling water and slowly heat to boiling.

Dice pork very fine. Pan-fry until crisp and light brown. Turn pork and remaining reside from pan into greens. Add salt, sugar and pepper and cook, covered, over low heat, for 30 minutes. Makes 4 servings.

MUSTARD GREENS AND SPINACH WITH BACON

(Southern Style)

2 lb. fresh tender mustard greens
½ lb. spinach
3 strips bacon

1 qt. boiling water
½ tsp. salt
¼ tsp. pepper

Wash mustard greens and spinach thoroughly. Chop into pieces. Put mustard greens into large pot with bacon. Add water. Cover and boil gently for 30 minutes. Add salt and pepper and put spinach in, pressing down well. Again, cover and cook until spinach is tender, from 10 to 15 minutes. Serve piping hot. Makes 4 servings.

GARDEN AND VEGETABLE PASTA

1 lb. pasta (any shape)
1 (1 lb.) bag frozen vegetables
1 c. low-fat sour cream

1 (1 oz.) pkg. garden vegetable
party dip
grated Parmesan cheese

Cook pasta in large pot of boiling water. About 5 minutes before pasta is done, stir in frozen vegetables. While they cook, in a large serving bowl, mix sour cream with dip packet. Drain pasta and vegetables well. Add to the sour cream mixture. Toss to cont. Serve with grated Parmesan cheese. Serves 4.

POTATO CASSEROLE

8 large potatoes
8 oz. pkg. cream cheese
1 c. sour cream

½ tsp. pepper
2 tsp. garlic or onion salt
4 Tbsp. margarine

Peel and cut up potatoes. Cook until done and mash well. Add softened cream cheese, sour cream, salt and pepper. Mix well.

Put into 9 x 12-inch pan. Dot with margarine. Bake, covered, at 400for 55 minutes.

SLICED BAKED POTATOES

4 medium potatoes
1 tap. Salt
2 to 3 Tbsp. melted butter

2 Tbsp. chopped fresh parsley
4 Tbsp. grated Cheddar cheese
1 ½ Tbsp. Parmesan cheese

Scrub unpeeled potatoes and rinse. Cut into thin slices, but not all the way through. Use a handle of a spoon to prevent knife from cutting all the way.

Put potatoes in a baking dish. Fan them slightly. Sprinkle with salt and drizzle with butter. Sprinkle with herbs.

Bake potatoes at 425° for about 50 minutes. Remove from oven. Sprinkle with cheeses. Bake potatoes for another 10 to 15 minutes until lightly browned, cheeses are melted and potatoes are soft inside. Check with a fork.

BEST BROCCOLI CASSEROLE

1 c. water
½ tsp. salt
1 c. instant
¼ c. butter
¼ chopped onion
¼ c' chopped celery

1 (10 ¾ oz.) can condensed
cream of mushroom soup
1 (1o ¾ oz.) can condensed
cream of celery soup
1 (1o oz.) pkg. frozen, chopped
broccoli, thawed
½ c. diced Cheddar cheese

Bring water and salt to a boil. Add rice. Cover and remove from heat. Let sit for 5 minutes. Melt butter in skillet. Sauté onion and celery until tender

In large mixing bowl, combine rice, celery and onion with remaining ingredients. Pour into a greased 1 ½-quart casserole. Bake at 350° for 1 hour.

WESTERN BEANS

4 bacon strips, diced
1 large onion, chopped
1/3 c. water
1 1/3 c. water
2 Tbsp. Ketchup
1 (16 oz,) can chopped whole
Tomatoes with liquid
1 (15 oz.) can pinto beans, Drained

1 (16 oz.) can kidney been
drained
¾ tsp. chili powder
1 tsp. garlic powder
½ tsp. ground cumin
¼ tsp. red pepper flakes
1 bay leaf

Lightly fry bacon in heavy 3-quart saucepan. Add onion. Cook until transparent. Stir in remaining ingredients. Cook over medium heat for 45 minutes or until lentils are tender, stirring once or twice. Remove bay leaf before serving.

SAUERKRAUT CASSROLE

1 lb. mild Italian sausage links,
Cut into 1-inch slices
1 large onion, chopped
2 apples, peeled and quartered

1 (27 oz.) can sauerkraut,
undrained
1 c. water
½ c. packed brown sugar
2 tsp. caraway seed

In skillet, cook sausage and onion until sausage is brown and onion is tender; drain. Stir in apples, sauerkraut, water, brown sugar and caraway seed.

Transfer to a 2 ½-quart baking dish. Cover and bake at 350° for 1 hour. Garnish with parsley.

CONFETTI SCALLOPED POTATOES

½ c. butter or margarine
½ c. chopped onion
1 (16 oz.) pkg. frozen hash brown
Potatoes
1 (10 ¾ oz.) can condensed
Cream of mushroom soup
1 c. milk

1 c. shredded Cheddar cheese
1 small green pepper, cut into
strips
2 Tbsp. chopped pimiento
dash of pepper
1 c. cheese cracker crumbs,
divided

In skillet, melt butter over medium heat. Saute onion until tender. Stir in potatoes, soup and milk. Add cheese, green pepper, pimiento, pepper and ½ cup of the crumbs.

Pour into a shallow casserole. Top with remaining crumbs, Bake at 375° for 35 to 40 minutes. Makes 6 to 8 servings.

GLAZED SWEET POTATOES

2 Tbsp. brown sugar
1 tsp. cornstarch
¼ tsp. ground ginger
½ c. apple juice

1 tsp. prepared mustard
1 (18 oz.) can sweet potatoes
1/3 c. cashews

In saucepan, mix brown sugar, cornstarch, ginger and ¼ tea-spoon salt. Add apple juice and mustard. Cook and stir until bubbly. Cook and stir 2 minutes more.

Drain sweet potatoes; stir into sugar mixture. Heat through. Stir in cashews. Serves 4.

GLAZED SWEET POTATOES

2 lb. sweet potatoes

¼ c. butter or margarine

¼ c. packed brown sugar

¼ tsp. ground cinnamon

Place potatoes in kettle. Cover with water and cook just until tender, about 35 minutes. Drain. Cool slightly. Peel and cut into slices. Place potatoes in 2-quart baking dish.

In small saucepan, combine butter, syrup, brown sugar and cinnamon. Cook and stir until mixture boils. Pour over potatoes. Bake at 350° for 30 to 40 minutes or until heated through.

Breads, Rolls & Pastries

Baking Tips

COMMON PROBLEMS (Common Failures)	CAYSES OF PROBLEMS (Causes of Failures)
Biscuits	
Rough biscuits	Insufficient mixing
Dry biscuits	Baking in too slow an oven and handling too much
Uneven browning	Cooking in dark surface pan, too high a temperature and rolling the dough too thin
Breads(yeast)	
Porous bread	Over-rising or cooking at too low a temperature
Crust is dark and blisters Just under the crust	Under-rising
Bread does not rise	Over-kneading or using old yeast
Bread is streaked	Under-kneading and not kneading evenly
Bread bakes unevenly	Using old, dark pans, too much sough in pan, crowding the oven shelf or cooking at too high a temperature
Cakes	
Cracks and uneven surface	Too much flour, too hot an oven and sometimes from cold oven start
Dry cakes	Too much flour, too little shortening too much baking powder or cooking at too low a temperature
Heavy cakes	Too much sugar or baking too short a period
Sticky crust	Too much sugar
Coarse grained cake	Too little mixing, too much shortening, too much baking powder, using shortening too soft, and baking at too low a temperature
Fallen cakes	Using insufficient flour, under baking, too much sugar, too much shortening or not enough baking powder
Uneven color	Cooking at too high a temperature, crowding the shelf (allow at least 2 inches around pans) or using dark pans
Uneven browning	Not mixing well

Cookies

Uneven browning	Not using shiny cookie sheet or not allowing at least 2 inches on all sides of cookie sheets in oven
Soggy Cookies	Cooling cookies in pans instead of racks
Excessive spreading of cookies	Dropping cookies onto hot cookie sheets; not chilling dough; not baking at correct temperature

Muffins

Coarse texture	Insufficient stirring and cooking at too low a temperature
Tunnels in muffins, peaks in center and soggy texture	Over-mixing

Pies

Pastry crumbles	Over-mixing flour and shortening
Pastry tough	Using too much water and over-mixing the dough
Pies do not brown (fruit or Custard)	Bake at constant temperature (400-425 degrees) in Pyrex or enamel pie pan

BREADS, ROLLS & PASTRIES

BASIC WHITE BREAD

1 c. milk
3 Tbsp. honey
2 tsp. salt
¼ c. butter or margarine

1 ¼ c. very warm water (but not hot)
2 Tbsp. active dry yeast
6 to 7 c. sifted flour

In saucepan, heat milk to simmering. Add honey, salt and butter. Cool to lukewarm. Measure water into larger bowl; add yeast and stir until dissolved. Stir in milk mixture. Add half of flour; beat until smooth, about 2 minutes. Gradually add remaining flour.

Knead on lightly floured board until smooth and elastic, 10 minutes. Place in lightly oiled bowl. Turn dpugh to oil top. Cover with towel. Let rise in warm place in lightly oiled bowl. Turn dough to oil top. Cover with towel. Let rise in warm place about 1 hour.

Punch down. Turn out onto lightly floured board. Divide in half and shape each portion into a loaf. Place in loaf pans.

Brush with butter. Cover with towel. Let rise in warm place, free from drafts, for about 1 hour. Bake in preheated oven at 375° for 40 to 45 minutes. Makes 2 loaves.

NO-KNEAD DROP ROLLS

2/3 c. sugar
¼ c. lukewarm water
1 pkg. dry yeast
1 c. milk, scalded and cooled

3 ½ c. all-purpose flour
1/3 c. shortening
3 eggs, beaten
1 tsp. vanilla

Stir 1 teaspoon of the sugar into water. Add yeast and let stand 10 minutes. Stir yeast mixture and add lukewarm milk, blend well. Add 1 ½ cups of the flour and beat until smooth. Cover and let batter rise in a warm place until light, about 45 minutes.

Cream shortening with salt and remaining sugar and add yeast batter gradually, stirring to mix well. Add eggs and vanilla and beat thoroughly. Add remaining flour and beat until thoroughly mixed.

Drop batter into well-greased muffin pans, filling about 1/3 full. Cover and allow to rise in a warm place until light, about 1 hour.

Brush lightly with melted butter and sprinkle with a mixture of 3 tablespoons of sugar and 1 teaspoon of cinnamon. Bake in a moderately hot oven (400°) for about 18 minutes. Makes about 2 dozen rolls.

BANANA SQUARES

2 eggs, separated
2/3 c. shortening
1 ½ c. sugar
1 c. mashed rips bananas (2 to 3 Medium)
1 ½ c. all-purpose flour

1 tsp. baking soda
¼ c. sour milk*
½ tsp. Vanilla
½ c. chopped walnuts
whipped cream

In small bowl, beat egg whites until soft peaks form; set aside. Ina large mixing bowl, cream shortening and sugar. Beat in egg yolks; mix well. Add bananas. Combine flour and baking soda; add to creamed mixture alternately with milk, beating well after each addition. Add vanilla. Fold in egg whites. Fold in nuts, if desired.

Pour into a greased 13 x 9 x 2-inch baking pan. Bake at 350° for 45 to 50 minutes. Cool on a wire rack. Garnish with whipped cream and banana slices.

*To sour milk, place 1 teaspoon white vinegar in a measuring cup. Add enough milk to equal 1/4 cup.

BANANA BREAD PUDDING

4 c. cubed, day-old French or Sourdough bread (1-inch pieces)
¼ c. butter or margarine, melted
3 eggs
2 c. milk
½ c. sugar

2 tsp. vanilla
½ tsp. cinnamon
½ tsp. nutmeg
½ tap salt
1 c. sliced firm bananas (1/4-inch Pieces)

Sauce:

3 Tbsp. butter or margarine
2 Tbsp. Sugar
1 Tbsp. cornstarch

¾ c. milk
¼ c. light corn syrup
1 tsp. vanilla

Place bread cubes in a greased 2-quart casserole. Pour butter over and toss to coat. In medium bowl, lightly beat eggs. Add milk, sugar, vanilla cinnamon, nutmeg and salt. Stir in bananas. Pour over bread cubes and stir to coat. Bake, uncovered, at 375° for 40 minutes or until a knife inserted near the center comes out clean.

Meanwhile, for sauce, melt butter in a small saucepan. Combine sugar and cornstarch; add to butter. Stir in milk and corn syrup. Cook and stir over medium heat until the mixture comes to a full boil. Boil for 1 minute. Remove from the heat. Stir in vanilla serve warm sauce over warm pudding.

APRICOT BANANA BREAD

1/3 c. butter or margarine, Softened
2/3 c. sugar
2 eggs
1 c. mashed ripe bananas (2 to 3 Medium)
¼ c. buttermilk
1 ¼ c. all-purpose flour

1 tsp. baking powder
½ tsp. baking soda
½ tsp. salt
1 c. 100%bran cereal (not flakes)
¾ c. chopped, dried apricots (6 oz.)
½ c. chopped walnuts

In mixing bowl, cream butter and sugar. Add eggs; mix well. Combine bananas and buttermilk. Combine the flour, baking powder, baking soda and salt; add to creamed mixture alternately with banana mixture. Stir in bran, apricots and nuts.

Pour into a greased 9 x 5 x 3-inch loaf pan. Bake at 350° for 55 to 60 minutes or until bread test done. Cool 10 minutes before removing from pan to a wire rack. Makes 1 loaf.

NUTTY BANANA BREAD

1 stick butter, softened
1 c. sugar
3 eggs
3 ½ c. flour
4 tsp. baking powder

2 tsp. salt
3 very ripe medium bananas, mashed
1 ½ c. chopped walnuts

Preheat oven to 325°. Grease two 9 x 5-inch loaf and dust lightly with flour.

Cream butter with sugar in a large mixing bowl. Beat in eggs, one at a time, mixing well after each addition. Sift together flour, baking powder and salt. Fold into butter mixture. Fold in bananas and chopped nuts.

Divide batter evenly between prepared pans, filling each slightly more than half full. Smooth tops, using a plastic spatula.

Bake for 40 minutes or until top is golden brown and toothpick inserted in center comes out clean. Cool on wire racks before removing from pans. Slice to desired thickness. Makes 2 loaves.

SWEET POTATO QUICK BREAD

2 1/3 c. sugar

2/3 c. water

2/3 c. oil

4 eggs, beaten

1 (23 oz.) can sweet potatoes in

Syrup, drained and mashed (2 c.)

3 ½ c. all-purpose flour

2 tsp. baking soda

1 ½ tsp. salt

1 tsp. cinnamon

½ tsp. baking powder

1 c. chopped pecans

Heat oven to 350°. Grease and flour two 9 x 5-inch loaf pans.

In large bowl, combine sugar, water, oil eggs and sweet potatoes; mix well. IN medium bowl, combine flour, baking soda, salt cinnamon and baking powder; mix well. Add flour mixture to sweet potato mixture. By hand, mix until well combined. Stir in pecans.

Pour evenly into greased and floured pans. Bake at 350° for 60 to70 minutes or until toothpick inserted in center comes out clean. Cool 15 minutes. Remove from pans. Cool completely.

COUNTRY APPLE COFFEE CAKE

2 Tbsp. butter, softened

1 ½ c. chopped, peeled apples

1 (10 oz.) can Hungry Jack

Refrigerated flaky biscuits

1/3 c. firmly packed brown sugar

¼ tsp. Cinnamon

1/3 c. light corn syrup

1 egg

½ c. pecan pieces or halves

Using 1 tablespoon of the butter, generously grease 9-inch round cake pan or 8-inch square pan. Spread 1 cup of the apples in greased pan.

Separate dough into 10 biscuits. Cut each into quarters. Arrange biscuit pieces, points up, over apples. Top with remaining ½ cup apples.

In small bowl, combine remaining 1 tablespoon butter, brown sugar, cinnamon, corn syrup and egg. Beat 2 to 3 minutes or until sugar is partially dissolved. Stir in pecans. Spoon over biscuit pieces and apples.

Bake at 350° for 35 to 45 minutes or until deep golden brown. Cool 5 minutes.

In small bowl, blend all glaze ingredients, adding enough milk for desired drizzling consistency. Drizzle over warm cake. Serve warm. Makes 6 to 8 servings.

CINNAMON COFFEE CAKE

1 C. Butter, softened
2 ¾ c. sugar, divided
2 tsp. vanilla
4 eggs
3 c. all-purpose flour
2 tsp. baking powder

1 tsp. baking soda
1 tsp. salt
2 c. (16 oz.) sour cream
2 Tbsp. cinnamon
½ c. chopped walnuts

In large mixing bowl, cream butter and 2 cups sugar until fluffy. Add vanilla. Add eggs, one at a time, beating well after each addition. Combine flour, baking powder, soda and salt; add alternately with sour cream, beating just enough after each addition to keep batter smooth.

Spoon 1/3 of batter into a greased 10-inch tube pan. Combine cinnamon, nuts and remaining sugar; sprinkle 1/3 over batter in pan. Repeat layers two more times.

Bake at 350° for 70 minutes or until cake test done. Cool for 10 minutes. Remove from pan to a wire rack to cool completely.

CHEDDAR APPLE BREAD

½ c. butter, softened
2 eggs, slightly beaten
1 tsp. vanilla
2 c. all-purpose flour
2/3 c. white sugar
1 tsp. baking powder
1 tsp. cinnamon

½ tsp. baking soda
½ tsp. cheese-flavored salt
½ tsp. nutmeg
2 c. peeled and shredded apples
¾ c. chopped walnuts
½ c. shredded sharp Cheddar
cheese

Combine butter, eggs and vanilla; mix well. Blend in dry ingredients; mix well. Fold in apples, walnuts and cheese.

Pour batter into a greased 9 x 5 x3-inch loaf pan. Bake at 350° for 55 to 60 minutes or until bread tests done. Remove to wire rack to cool.

CRANBERRY ORANGE BREAD

2 c. all-purpose flour
1 ½ tsp. baking powder
1 tsp. baking soda
½ tsp. salt
1 c. sugar
1 egg, beaten

½ c. orange juice
grated rind of orange
2 Tbsp. melted butter
2 Tbsp. hot water
1 c. raw whole cranberries
1 c. chopped walnuts

Combine flour, baking powder, soda, salt and sugar in large mixing bowl. Set aside. Mix beaten egg with orange juice, rind, butter and hot water. Fold flour mixture into egg mixture until blended. Do not beat. Gently fold in cranberries and walnuts.

Spoon into a greased 9 x 6 x 3-inch loaf pan. Bake at 325° for 60 minutes. Test in center with toothpick. Cool on rack for 15 minutes before removing from pan.

CRANBERRY PUMPKIN BREAD

2 eggs, beaten
1 c. white sugar
½ c. vegetable oil
1 tsp. butter flavor extract
1 c. canned or cooked pumpkin

2 ¼ c. all-purpose flour
1 Tbsp. pumpkin pie spice
1 tsp. baking soda
¼ tsp. salt
1 c. chopped cranberries

Combine first 5 ingredients; mix well. In large bowl, blend flour, pumpkin pie spice, soda and salt. Stir in pumpkin mixture just until dry ingredients are moistened. Stir in cranberries.

Spoon batter into 9 x 5-inch loaf pan. Bake at 350° for 75 minutes or until bread tests done. Cool in pan on rack for 10 minutes. Remove from pan and cool completely.

POTATO REFRIGERATOR DOUGH

1 pkg. dry yeast
1 ½ c. warm water
2/3 c. shortening
2/3 c. sugar

1 ½ tsp. salt
2 eggs
1 c. lukewarm mashed potatoes
7 to 7 ½ c. all-purpose flour

Dissolve yeast in warm water. Stir in shortening, sugar, salt, eggs, potatoes and 4 cups flour. Beat until smooth. Mix in enough remaining flour to make dough easy to handle.

Turn onto lightly floured board. Knead until smooth and elastic, about 5 minutes. Place in greased bowl; turn greased side up. Cover tightly. Refrigerate at least 6 hours or until ready to use. Can be kept for 5 days in refrigerator.

Punch dough down; divide in half. Use one-half for Cinnamon Swirl cake. Return remaining half to refrigerator until ready to use.

Cinnamon Swirl Cake:

½ Potato Refrigerator Dough (in
2 parts)
¼ c. butter, softened
½ c. sugar

½ c. chopped walnuts
½ c. raisins
1 Tbsp. plus 1 tsp. ground
cinnamon

Roll ½ of dough in rectangle,1/4inch thick. Spread with softened butter. Mix sugar. Nuts, raisins and cinnamon. Sprinkle half the mixture on the rectangle. Roll up jelly roll fashion. Pinch ends of dough into roll to seal well. Stretch roll to make even and about 12 inches long. Cut into 12 (1-inch) slices.

Line a 10-inch tube pan with foil and grease lightly. Arrange 6 slices of dough with cut sides against outer side of pan. Arrange 6 slices with cut sides up in bottom of pan. Sprinkle with remaining cinnamon mixture. Cover. Let rise in warm place until double, 1 ½ to 2 hours.

Bake 445 minutes at 375°. Drizzle warm cake with Sugar Glaze.

Sugar Glaze:

1 c. confectioners' sugar
1 Tbsp. plus 1 tsp. milk

½ tsp. vanilla flavoring

Mix together until smooth. Add more milk, if needed. Drizzle over warm cake.
Note: If cake becomes too brown while baking, cover with a piece of aluminum foil.

SPICED APPLESAUCE BREAD

1 ¼ c. unsweetened applesauce
1 c. white sugar
½ vegetable oil
2 eggs
3 Tbsp. milk
2 tsp. cinnamon apple extract
1 tsp. vanilla
2 c. all-purpose flour
1 tsp. baking soda

½ tsp. baking powder
½ tsp. cinnamon
¼ tsp. nutmeg
¼ tsp. salt
½ c. chopped pecans or walnuts
¼ c. finely chopped pecans or walnuts
¼ c. brown sugar
½ tsp. pumpkin pie spice

Thoroughly combine the first 7 ingredients. Add the 6 dry ingredients and beat well. Fold in the ½ cup nuts. Turn into well-greased and floured 9 x 5-inch loaf pan.

Combine the ¼ cup nuts, brown sugar and pumpkin pie spice, sprinkle over batter. Bake at 350° for 60 to 75 minutes. Cool 10 minutes. Remove from pan and cool completely.

SPICY PEACH BREAD

2 c. all-purpose flour
2/3 c. white sugar
2 Tbsp. baking powder
2 tsp. cinnamon
½ tsp. nutmeg
½ tsp. ground cloves
½ tsp. salt

2 Tbsp. butter
1 (16 oz.) can sliced peaches in syrup (drain and reserve syrup)
½ c. reserved peach syrup
2 eggs, beaten
1 tsp. vanilla
½ tsp. peach flavor extract

Place all ingredients in large mixing bowl and beat for 2 minutes, pour into greased 9x5-inch loaf pan and bake at 350° for 55 to 65 minutes or until bread tests done.

Remove from pan immediately and cool completely on wire rack. When cool, drizzle with glaze. Store tightly wrapped in refrigerator.

Powdered Sugar Glaze:

½ c. powdered sugar
¼ tsp. white vanilla flavoring

1 to 2 tsp. hot milk

Combine powdered sugar, vanilla and enough of the milk to get a smooth glaze. Drizzle over bread.

CARAMEL BISCUIT RING-A-ROUND

3/4 c. packed brown sugar
½ c. chopped nuts
1/3 c. butter

2 Tbsp. water
2 cans flaky biscuits

Separate biscuits into 20. Cut each biscuit into ¼-inch pieces.

Mix packed brown sugar, nuts, butter and water. Heat until butter melts. Put biscuits into large bowl. Pour brown sugar mixture over biscuits. Toss lightly to coat biscuits evenly. Spoon into pan.

Bake in 400° oven for 20 to 30 minutes. Use a greased, fluted pan. Let stand 3 minutes. Invert onto serving plate.

BAKLAVA

1 lb. file dough

Filling:

¼ lb. melted unsweetened butter
2 c. chopped pecans
2 c. chopped walnuts

1 c. sugar
1 tsp. cinnamon

Keep filo dough covered with moist cheesecloth, while making, to keep dough from drying out. For filling, combine butter, pecans, walnuts, sugar and cinnamon.

Start out with 8 sheets filo; butter each sheet. Add filling, Place layer after layer with filling between each sheet, Cut into diamonds or squares before baking. Bake on cookie sheet at 325° for one hour.

Syrup:

2 c. sugar
2 c. water

juice of ½ lemon

Combine and heat on low heat for 15 minutes. While still hot, pour syrup overall.

MAGIC MARSHMALLOW CRESCENT PUFFS

Puffs:

¼ c. sugar

2 Tbsp. flour

1 tsp. cinnamon

2 (8 oz.) cans refrigerated
crescent dinner rolls

16 large marshmallows

¼ c. butter or margarine, melted

Glaze:

½ c. powdered sugar

½ tsp. vanilla

2 to 3 Tbsp. milk

¼ c. chopped nuts (if desired)

Puffs: In small bowl, combine sugar, flour and cinnamon. Separate dough into 16 triangles. Dip I1 marshmallow in margarine; Roll in sugar mixture. Place marshmallow on wide end of triangle and roll to opposite point. Completely cover marshmallow with dough, firmly pinch edges to seal. Dip one end in remaining margarine.

Place, margarine side down, in ungreased large muffin cup or 6-ounce custard cup. Repeat with remaining marshmallows.

Bake at 375° for 12 to 15 minutes or until golden brown. Immediately remove from muffin cups. Cool on wire racks over waxed paper.

Glaze: In small bowl, blend powdered sugar, vanilla and enough milk for desired drizzling consistency. Drizzle over warm rolls. Sprinkle with nuts. Makes 16 rolls.

ALMOND FILLED COOKIE CAKE

Crust:

2 2/3 c. all-purpose flour   ½ tsp. salt

1 1/3 c. sugar   1 egg

1 1/3 c. butter, softened (do not use margarine)

Filling:

1 c. finely chopped almonds   1 egg, slightly beaten

½ c. sugar   4 whole blanched almonds

1 tsp. grated lemon peel

Heat oven to 325°. Place cookie sheet in oven to preheat. Grease 9 or 10-inch spring-form pan.

Lightly spoon flour into measuring cup; level off. In large bowl, blend all crust ingredients at low speed until dough forms. If desired, refrigerate for easier handling

Divide dough in half; spread half in bottom of greased pan to form crust. In small bowl, combine all filling ingredients, except whole almonds; blend well. Spread over crust to within ½ inch of sides of pan.

Between 2 sheets of waxed paper, press remaining dough to 9 or10-inch circle. Remove top sheet of waxed paper. Place dough over filling. Remove waxed paper. Press dough into place. Top with whole almonds.

Place cake on preheated cookie sheet. Bake at 325° for 65 to 75 minutes or until top is light golden brown. Cool 15 minutes. Remove sides of pan. Cool completely. Yields 24 servings.

CREAM PUFFS

½ c. Bolling water

¼ c. butter

½ c. all-purpose flour

2 eggs

Pour boiling water over butter in a saucepan. Heat just to boiling and stir until butter melts. Sift flour; measure. Add all at once to the butter mixture. Stir constantly with a wooden spoon until the mixture leaves the sides of the pan and forms a ball.

Remove from heat. Immediately add unbeaten eggs, one at a time, beating to a smooth paste after each one. Then beat the mixture until smooth and velvety. Drop by heaping tablespoonfuls onto a greased baking sheet, keeping about 3 inches apart.

Bake in a hot oven (450°) for 15 minutes or until well puffed and delicately browned. Then reduce the heat to 300° and bake for 30 to 40 minutes longer. This will cook the centers thoroughly, but puffs should become no browner.

Remove to a cake rack to cool. When cold, cut off tops with a sharp knife. Fill with Cream Filling, whipped cream or ice cream and replace tops. Makes 6 to 7 puffs.

Cream Filling for Cream Puffs:

½ c. sugar

¼ c. flour

½ tsp. salt

1 ½ c. milk, scalded

1 egg, beaten

1 ½ Tbsp. butter

1 tsp. vanilla

Mix sugar, flour and salt in top of double boiler. Gradually stir in ¾ cup of the hot milk. Stir until smooth. Add the remaining milk and cook over direct heat until thickened, stirring constantly. Stir a little of the hot mixture into the beaten egg. Return this to rest of mixture and place over boiling water, stirring constantly, for 2 minutes. Remove from heat. Stir in butter and flavoring. Cool. Fill into cream puffs.

SPOON BREAD

1 pt. sweet milk
6 Tbsp. butter
1 c. cornmeal

1 tsp. salt
3 eggs

Scald milk (do not boil). Stir in butter, cornmeal and salt, Cook, stirring constantly, until cornmeal comes away from sides of pan and thickens. Set aside to cool until lukewarm. Add beaten egg yolks. Mix thoroughly. Fold in stiffly beaten egg whites. Mix gently, but thoroughly.

Pour into greased and floured 2-quart baking dish. Bake at 375° for 1 hour or until top is golden brown. Serve immediately.

MAMA'S CORNBREAD

1 ½ c. yellow cornmeal
½ c. flour
4 tsp. baking powder
½ tsp. salt

¼ c. sugar
1 c. milk
1 egg, beaten
¼ c. oil

Mix cornmeal, flour, baking powder, salt and sugar. Mix together milk and egg. Add milk mixture to dry mixture.

Melt oil in skillet. Stir into cornbread mixture. Bake at 425° for approximately 25 minutes.

CRACKLIN' CORNBREAD

2 c. yellow cornmeal
2 tsp. baking powder
1 tsp. baking soda
¾ tsp. salt

2 eggs, beaten
2 c. buttermilk
2 Tbsp. vegetable oil
1 c. cracklings

Combine cornmeal, baking powder, soda and salt in a large bowl. Add eggs, buttermilk, oil and cracklings, stirring just until dry ingredients are moistened.

Place a well-greased cast-iron skillet in a 450° oven for 4 minutes or until hot. Remove from oven, spoon batter into skillet. Bake at 450° for 25 minutes or until lightly browned. Makes 8 servings.

CORNMEAL PANCAKES

1 c. yellow cornmeal
¼ c. flour
½ tsp. salt

2 Tbsp. oil
1 tsp. brown sugar
2 eggs, beaten

Mix together cornmeal, flour and salt. Add ¼ cup boiling water slowly, stirring all the time. Add a little more water, if necessary, to make a medium batter. Blend in oil and sugar. Beat in eggs until mixed well. Cook on ungreased griddle.

CORNMEAL SESAME BATTER ROLLS

1 ¾ to 2 c. all-purpose flour
½ c. yellow or white cornmeal
1 Tbsp. sugar
1 tsp. salt
1 pkg. active dry yeast

1 c. milk
¼ c. butter
1 egg
sesame seed

Well-grease 12 muffin cups. Lightly spoon flour into measuring cup; level off. In large bowl, combine 1 cup flour, cornmeal, sugar, salt and yeast: blend well.

In small saucepan, heat milk and margarine until very warm (120° to 130°). Add warm liquid and egg to flour mixture. Blend at low speed until moistened, 2 minutes at medium speed. By hand, stir in ¾ to 1 cup flour to form a stiff dough. Over batter. Let rise in warm place until light and doubled in size, about 45 minutes.

Stir down dough. Spoon into prepared muffin cups. Sprinkle with sesame seed. Cover. Let rise in warm place until light and doubled in size, about 30 minutes.

Heat oven to 400°. Bake 10 to 15 minutes or until golden brown. Remove from pan immediately. Makes 12 rolls.

ANGEL BISCUITS

2 pkg. active dry yeast
¼ c. warm water (110° to 115°)
2 c. warm buttermilk (110° to 115°)
5 c. all-purpose flour
1/3 c. sugar

1 Tbsp. baking powder
1 tsp. baking soda
1 Tbsp. salt
1 c. shortening
melted butter or margarine

Dissolve yeast in warm water. Let stand 5 minutes. Stir in buttermilk. Set aside.

In large mixing bowl, combine flour, sugar, baking powder, soda and salt. Cut in shortening with pastry blender or butter knife until mixture resembles coarse meal. Stir in yeast/buttermilk mixture; mix well.

Turn out onto a lightly floured surface. Knead lightly 3 to 4 times. Roll to a 1/2-inch thickness. Cut with a 2 ½-inch biscuit cutter. Place on a lightly greased baking sheet. Cover and let rise in a warm place about 1 ½ hours.

Bake at 450° for 8 to 10 minutes. Lightly brush tops with melted butter. Makes about 2 ½ dozen.

MOM'S BUTTERMILK BISCUITS

2 c. all-purpose flour
2 tsp. baking powder
½ tsp. baking soda

½ tsp. salt
¼ c. shortening
¾ c. buttermilk

In a bowl, combine the flour, baking powder, baking soda and salt. Cut in shortening until the mixture resembles coarse crumbs. Stir in buttermilk.

Knead dough gently. Roll out to ½-inch thickness. Cut with a 2-inch biscuit cutter.

Place on a lightly greased baking sheet. Bake at 450° for 10 to 15 minutes or until golden brown.

FARMHOUSE BARBECUE MUFFINS

1 (1o oz.) can refrigerated
Buttermilk biscuits
1 lb. ground beef
½ c. ketchup
3 Tbsp. brown sugar

1 Tbsp. cider vinegar
½ tsp. chili powder
1 c. (4 oz.) shredded Cheddar
cheese

Separate dough into 10 biscuits; flatten into 5-inch circles. Press each into the bottom and up the sides of a greased muffin cup; set aside.

In a skillet, brown ground beef; drain. In a small bowl, mix ketchup, brown sugar, vinegar and chili powder; stir until smooth. Add to meat and mix well.

Divide the meat mixture among biscuit-lined muffin cups, using about ¼ cup for each. Sprinkle with cheese.

Bake at 375° for 18 to 20 minutes or until golden brown. Cool for 5 minutes before removing from tin and serving.

FEATHER-LIGHT MUFFINS

1/3 c. shortening
½ c. sugar
1 egg
1 ½ c. cake flour

1 ½ tsp. baking powder
½ tsp. salt
¼ tsp. nutmeg
½ c. milk

Topping:

½ c. sugar
1 tsp. cinnamon

½ c. butter or margarine, melted

In mixing bowl, cream shortening, sugar and egg. Combine dry ingredients; add to creamed mixture alternately with milk.

Fill greased muffin tins 2/3 full. Bake at 325° for 20 to 25 minutes or until golden. Let cool for 3 to 4 minutes.

Topping: Meanwhile, combine sugar and cinnamon in a small bowl. Roll warm muffins in melted butter, then in sugar mixture. Serve warm. Makes 8 to 10 muffins.

FRUIT MUFFINS

2 c. all-purpose flour
1 tsp. baking soda
½ tsp. cinnamon
¼ tsp. nutmeg
1/8 tsp. cloves
2/3 c. shortening

½ c. packed brown sugar
2 eggs
½ c. dairy sour cream
½ c. milk
1 (8 ¼ oz) can crushed
pineapple, drained

Mix first five ingredients and ¼ teaspoon salt. In mixer bowl, beat shortening and brown sugar until fluffy. Beat in eggs, sour cream and milk. Stir in flour mixture. Fold in pineapple.

Fill greased muffin tins 2/3 full. Bake in a 350° oven for 25 to 30 minutes. Makes 12 to 14 muffins.

BLUEBERRY MUFFINS

1 ¾ c. all-purpose flour
1/3 c. sugar
2 ½ tsp. baking powder
½ tsp. salt
1 egg

1 c. fresh or unthawed frozen
blueberries
¾ c. milk
1/3 c. melted butter

In large bowl, combine flour, sugar, baking powder and salt. Stir in blueberries. Add milk, egg and butter. Mix just until dry ingredients are moistened. The batter will be lumpy. Do not overbeat.

Spoon batter into twelve greased muffin cups. Bake at 400° for 25 minutes or until tops spring back when lightly touched. Serve warm.

PEANUT BUTTER AND JELLY FRENCH TOAST

12 slices bread
¾ c. peanut butter
6 Tbsp. jelly or jam
3 eggs

¾ c. milk
¼ tsp. salt
2 Tbsp. butter or margarine

Spread peanut butter on six slices of bread; spread jelly on other six slices. Put one slice of each together to form sandwiches.

In mixing bowl, lightly beat eggs. Add milk and salt and mix together. Melt butter in large skillet over medium heat. Dip sandwiches in egg mixture, coating well. Place in skillet and brown on both sides. Serve immediately. Makes 6 sandwiches.

COTTAGE CHEESE APPLE PIE

Unbaked 0-inch pie shell
2 eggs
½ c. sugar
1/8 tsp. salt
½ c. cream, scalded
¾ c. milk, scalded

1 tsp. vanilla
1 c. cottage cheese
1 ½ c. tart apples, sliced thin
¼ c. sugar
¼ tsp. cinnamon
¼ tsp. nutmeg

Beat eggs slightly; add the one-half cup of sugar, salt, scalded cream and milk, vanilla and cottage cheese. Mix sliced apples with the one-fourth cup sugar and spices, adding more sugar if apples are very tart.

Turn apple mixture into unpricked pastry-lined pie pan. Bake in hot oven at 425° for 15 minutes. Reduce heat to 325°.

Pour custard mixture over top of apples and continue baking 40 minutes or until mixture sets and is a delicate brown in color. Cool on cake rack before cutting.

CREAMY BANANA PIE

1 (10-inch) baked pastry shell
1 envelope unflavored gelatin
¼ c. cold water
¾ c. sugar
¼ tsp. cornstarch
½ tsp. salt
2 ¼ c. milk

4 egg yolks, beaten
2 Tbsp, butter or margarine
1 Tbsp. vanilla
4 medium firm bananas
1 c. heavy cream, whipped
11/2 c. apple jelly

Soften gelatin in cold water; set aside. In saucepan, combine sugar, cornstarch and salt. Blend in the milk and egg yolks. Cook over low heat, stirring constantly, until thickened and bubbly, about 20 to 25 minutes.

Remove from heat. Stir in softened gelatin until dissolved. Stir in butter and vanilla. Cover the surface of the custard with plastic wrap and chill until no longer warm.

Slice 3 bananas; fold into custard with whipped cream. Spoon into pie shell. Chill until set, about 4 to 5 hours.

Shortly before serving time, place lemon juice in a small bowl and slice the remaining banana into it. Melt jelly in a saucepan over low heat. Drain banana; pat dry and arrange on top of pie. Brush banana with grated lemon peel. Serve immediately.

BUTTERSCOTCH PIE

Baked 8-inch pie shell
1 c. packed brown sugar
3 Tbsp. flour
4 ½ tsp. cornstarch
½ tsp. salt

1 ½ c. scalded milk
3 eggs, separated
3 Tbsp. butter
¾ tsp. vanilla
½ c. whipping cream

Mix sugar, flour, cornstarch, and salt thoroughly in top of double boiler. Add ¾ cup of the hot milk and stir over direct heat until smooth. Add ¾ cup of the hot milk and stir over direct heat until smooth. Add remaining milk, then place over boiling water and cook with frequent stirring for 15 minutes.

Beat egg whites until stiff and fold into the hot mixture and pour back into double boiler. Cook for 3 minutes longer, stirring constantly. Remove from heat. Add butter and vanilla and stir until mixed. Beat egg whites until stiff and fold into the hot mixture.

Pour immediately into cooled pie shell. When ready to serve, spread lightly with whipped cream.

LUSCIOUS LEMON MERINGUE PIE

Pastry for 1- crust pie

Lemon Filling:

¼ c. cornstarch

3 Tbsp. flour

1 ¾ c. sugar

¼ tsp. salt

4 egg yolks, slightly beaten

½ c. lemon juice

1 Tbsp. grated lemon peel

1 Tbsp. butter

Meringue:

4 egg whites

¼ tsp. cream of tartar

½ c. sugar

Bake pastry in 425° oven for 8 to 10 minutes. Be sure to prick entire surface with fork before baking. Cool on rack.

Make Lemon Filling: In medium saucepan, combine cornstarch, flour, 1 ¼ cups sugar and salt; mix well. Gradually add ½ cup sugar, stirring until smooth. Over medium heat, bring to boiling, stirring occasionally. Boil 1 minute until shiny and translucent.

Quickly stir some of the hot mixture into egg yolks. Pour back into hot mixture. Stir to blend. Return to heat. Cook over low heat for 5 minutes, stirring occasionally. Remove from heat. Stir in lemon juice, lemon rind and butter. Pour into pie shell.

Make Meringue: Beat whites with cream of tartar in medium bowl on medium speed until frothy. Beat in sugar, 2 tablespoons at a time, beating after each addition. Beat at high speed until stiff peaks form when beater is solely raised.

Spread meringue over Lemon Filling, carefully sealing to edge of the crust and swirling the top decoratively. Bake 7 to 9 minutes or until meringue is golden brown. Cool 2 to 3 hours on rack.

LEMON MERINGUE PIE

Baked 8-inch pie shell
¼ c. cornstarch
2 Tbsp. flour
1 ¼ c. sugar
¼ tsp. salt
1 ½ c. boiling water

4 eggs, separated
1/3 c. strained lemon juice
2 Tbsp. butter
½ tsp. grated lemon rind
1/3 c sugar

Blend cornstarch, flour, 1 ¼ cups sugar and salt in saucepan. Add boiling water gradually and blend thoroughly. Cook over direct heat, stirring constantly, boiling until thick and clear, about 3 minutes.

Beat egg yolks and stir in a little of the hot mixture. Pour back into saucepan. Stir to blend and cook two minutes longer with constant stirring. Remove from heat. Add lemon juice slowly in small portions, mixing well between each addition. Add butter and lemon rind, mixing well. Pour into cooled pie shell. Cool.

Beat the egg whites until stiff. Add the 1/3 cup sugar gradually and continue beating until thick and smooth. Pile lightly and quickly over pie filling to touch edges of crust all around.

Bake in a moderate oven (350°) for 12 to 15 minutes or until golden brown. Cool on cake rack before cutting.

CHERRY-RHUBARB PIE

Pastry for 2-crust pie, unbaked

Filling:

16 oz. pkg. frozen rhubarb,
Thawed and drained
16 oz. can pitted, tart, red
Cherries, drained

1 ½ c. sugar
2 Tbsp. tapioca

Heat oven to 400°. In large bowl, combine rhubarb, cherries, sugar and tapioca. Pour into pie crust pan. Top with second crust and flute. Slit crust in several place. Bake at 400° for 35 to 45 minutes or until golden brown.

PEACH 'N PRALINE PIE

1 (9-inch) pastry shell, unbaked

Filling:

¼ c. sugar
3 Tbsp. flour
¼ tsp. salt
¼ tsp. nutmeg
½ c. light corn syrup

Topping:

½ c. coarsely chopped pecans
¼ c. flour
¼ c. firmly packed brown sugar

1 tsp. flour

3 eggs
1 (29 oz.) can peach slices,
drained and cubed
¼ c. butter or margarine, melted

2 Tbsp. butter or margarine,
softened

Heat oven to 400°. In large bowl, combine sugar, flour, salt, nutmeg, corn syrup and eggs. Beat at medium speed 1 minute. Stir in peaches and margarine. Pour into pie crust-lined pan.

In small bowl, combine topping ingredients; mix well. Sprinkle over peach filling.

Bake at 400° for 35 to 45 minutes or until center is set. Cool. Garnish with whipped cream.

PEANUT BUTTER PIE

Crust:

1 ¼ c. chocolate cookie crumbs
(20 cookies)

Filling:

1 (8 oz.) pkg. cream cheese, Softened
1 c. creamy peanut butter
1 c. sugar

¼ c. sugar
¼ c. butter or margarine, melted

1 Tbsp. butter or margarine, softened
1 tsp. vanilla
1 c. heavy cream, whipped

Combine crust ingredients. Press into a 9-inch pie plate. Bake at 375° for 10 minutes. Cool.

In mixing bowl, beat cream cheese, peanut butter, sugar, butter and vanilla until smooth. Fold in whipped cream.

Gently spoon into crust. Garnish with chocolate or cookie crumbs, if desired. Refrigerate.

KENTUCKY PECAN PIE

Pastry for 9-inch pie
1 c. white corn syrup
1 c. brown sugar
1/8 tsp. salt

1/3 c. butter, melted
1 tsp. vanilla
3 whole eggs, beaten slightly
1 c. pecan halves

Combine syrup, sugar, salt, butter and vanilla; mix well. Add slightly beaten eggs. Pour into unbaked pie shell. Sprinkle pecans over top.

Bake in a preheated 350° oven for approximately 45 minutes. When cool, top with whipped cream.

PECAN PIE

1/3 c. butter or margarine
1 Tbsp. flour
1 ½ c. molasses
½ c. sugar

2 eggs
1 c. pecans
unbaked pastry for 8-inch pie

Melt the butter. Add flour and stir until smooth, then add molasses and sugar and boil 3 minutes. Cool. Add beaten eggs and nuts, blending well. Pour into pie shell. Bake at 350° for 40 minutes.

PERFECT PECAN PIE

Pastry for 8-inch pie
3 eggs
½ c. sugar
1 c. dark corn syrup

½ tsp. salt
1 tsp. vanilla
¼ c. melted butter or margarine
1 c. pecans

Beat the eggs, then add sugar, syrup, salt and vanilla. Add melted butter last. Place pecans on the bottom of unbaked pie crust. Add filling.

Bake in preheated 350° oven for 45 to 50 minutes. The pecans will rise to the top to form a crusted layer.

PUMPKIN PIE

1 ½ c. cooked pumpkin
1 ¼ c. molasses
½ tsp. salt
2 Tbsp. cornstarch
2 eggs, slightly beaten

1 ½ c. milk
1 tsp. cinnamon
¼ tsp. ginger
1 Tbsp. butter or margarine
unbaked pastry for 9-inch pie

Combine ingredients above in the order given and pour into pastry. Bake at 400° for 10 minutes, then reduce heat to 350° for 20 to 25 minutes, until custard is firm in center.

SKY-HIGH STRAWBERRY PIE

1 deep-dish pastry shell
(10-inch), baked
3 qt. fresh strawberries, divided
1 ½ c. sugar
6 Tbsp, cornstarch

2/3 c. water
1 c. heavy cream
1 ½ Tbsp. instant vanilla pudding mix

In large bowl, mash enough berries to equal 3 cups. In saucepan, combine the sugar and cornstarch. Stir in the mashed berries and water; mix well. Bring to a boil over medium heat, stirring constantly. Cook and stir for 2 minutes.

Remove from the heat. Pour into a large bowl. Chill for 20 minutes, stirring occasionally, until mixture is just slightly warm. Fold in the remaining berries. Pile into pie shell. Chill for 2 to 3 hours,

In a small mixing bowl, whip the cream until soft peaks form. Sprinkle puddings mix over cream and whip until stiff. Pipe around edge of pie or dollop on individual slices.

SWEET POTATO PIE

¼ c. molasses

½ c. sugar

½ tsp. salt

¾ tsp. cinnamon

¼ tsp. cloves

½ tsp. nutmeg

3 Tbsp. melted butter

1 ½ c. cooked sweet potatoes, mashed

3 eggs, separated

¾ c. milk

unbaked pastry for 9-inch pie

Add molasses, sugar, salt, spices and melted butter to mashed sweet potatoes. Mix thoroughly. Add well beaten egg yolks and milk. Mix well. Fold in stiffly beaten egg whites.

Pour into pastry shell. Bake in moderate oven at 350° for one hour or until a thin blade knife inserted in center of pie comes out clean.

SOULFUL SWEET POTATO PIE

Unbaked 8-inch pie shell

3 medium sweet potatoes

¼ c. butter, melted

2 eggs, separated

½ c. molasses

¼ tsp. salt

¼ tsp. nutmeg

1 tsp. baking powder

½ c. milk

1 tsp. grated orange rind

1 tsp. brandy flavored extract

Place potatoes in a saucepan. Cover with boiling water and cook until soft. Drain. Remove skins and mash thoroughly. Add melted butter, egg yolks, molasses, salt, nutmeg and baking powder and beat until smooth and creamy. Then stir in milk, orange rind and brandy extract.

Pour into the unpricked pie shell. Bake at 300° for about 45 minutes or until knife inserted in center comes out clean.

Remove pie from oven. Spread with meringue made by beating the 2 egg whites until stiff, then beating in 3 tablespoons sugar. Return to oven for 20 minutes to brown meringue, Cool on cake rack before cutting.

Cakes, Cookies & Desserts

Candy Testing

Candy	Degrees	Stage	Cold Water Test
	230-234	Thread	Syrup spins 2-inch thread when dropped from spoon
Fudge Fondant	234-240	Soft Ball	Candy will roll into a firm but quickly flattens when removed from water
Divinity Caramel's	244-248	Firm ball	Candy will roll into a firm ball (but not hard ball) which will not lose its shape upon removal from water
Taffy	250-266	Hard ball	Syrup forms hard ball, although it is pliable
Butterscotch	270-290	Light Crack	Candy will form threads in water which will soften when removed from water
Peanut Brittle	300-310	Hard Crack	Candy will form hard, threads in water which will not soften when removed from water
Caramelized Sugar	310-321	Caramelized	Sugar first melts then becomes a golden brown and forms a hard brittle ball in cold water

☐ CAKES, COOKIES & DESSERTS

OLDE ENGLISH APPLE CAKE

3 eggs
1 c. Crisco oil
1 ¾ c. sugar
2 c. flour, sifted

1 tsp. soda
1 tsp. cinnamon
5 apples, peeled and diced
1 ½ c. chopped walnuts

Mix eggs, oil and sugar. Sift flour, soda and cinnamon together. Add to egg mixture. Stir in apples and walnuts.

Pour into a greased and floured 9 x 13-inch pan. Bake at 350° for 50 minutes or until batter pulls away from sides of pan. Cool. Top with powdered sugar.

APPLESAUCE FRUITCAKE

1 ½ c. sugar
1 c. shortening
2 eggs
3 ¼ c. all-purpose flour
1 ½ tsp. soda
2 tsp. cinnamon
1 tsp. allspice
1 tsp. cloves
½ tsp. salt

1 ½ c. chopped nuts
1 1.2 c. raisins
1 ½ c. coarsely chopped dates
½ c. coarsely chopped
maraschino cherries, drained
2 c. applesauce
6 maraschino cherries, halved
6 pecan halves

Heat oven to 325°. Grease 10-inch tube pan. Line with waxed paper or foil. Grease waxed paper lining.

In large bowl, cream sugar and shortening until light and fluffy. Add eggs; mix well. Lightly spoon flour into measuring cup, level off. Reserve ½ cup flour. Add remaining 2 ¾ cups flour, soda, cinnamon, allspice, cloves and salt. Blend at low speed until moistened. Beat 2 minutes at medium speed.

Combine ½ cup reserved flour with nuts, raisins, dates and cherries. Stir until nuts and fruit are lightly coated. By hand, stir nut and fruit mixture and applesauce into batter. Mix well. Pour into prepared pan. Top with cherry halves and pecans.

Bake at 325° for 1 ¼ to 1 ¾ hours or until toothpick inserted in center comes out clean. Cool upright in pan 5 minutes. Remove from pan. Turn upright onto cooling rack. Remove paper. Cool completely.

Wrap cooled cake in plastic wrap or foil to keep moist. Store in refrigerator.

BEST EVER TROPICAL CAKE

1 box yellow
1 large can crushed pineapple,
Undrained
1 c. sugar

1 large box vanilla pudding mix
(not instant)
1 c. flaked coconut
1 (9 oz) container cool whip
1 c. chopped nuts

Bake cake in 13 x 8-inch greased and floured pan according to box directions. While cake is baking, simmer pineapple and sugar together.

Remove cake from oven and poke holes all over top with end of wooden spoon. Pour pineapple mix over cake. Prepare pudding mix per directions. Add coconut. Cool. Spread pudding over cake. Chill.

Before serving, cover with whipped topping and sprinkle with nuts.

COCONUT CARROT CAKE

2 c. unsifted all-purpose flour
2 ½ tsp. baking soda
2 tsp. cinnamon
1 tsp. salt
1 c. oil
2 c. sugar
3 eggs

1 (8 oz.) can crushed pineapple
in juice
2 c. grated carrots
½ c. chopped nuts
1 1/3 c. flaked or shredded
coconut

Combine flour, baking soda, cinnamon and salt; set aside. Beat oil, sugar and eggs until well blended. Add flour mixture; beat until smooth. Blend in remaining ingredients.

Pour into greased 10-inch tube pan or 13 x 9-inch pan. Bake at 350° for 50 to 55 minutes or until tester inserted in center comes out clean. Cool in pan 10 minutes. Remove from pan. Cool on rack. Frost with Coconut Cream Cheese Frosting.

Coconut Cream Cheese Frosting:

1 c. flaked or shredded coconut
1 ½ tsp. butter
1 (3 oz.) pkg. Cream cheese
¼ c. butter or margarine

3 c. sifted confectioners' sugar
1 Tbsp. milk
1 tsp. vanilla

Sauté coconut in 1 ½ teaspoons butter until golden brown, stirring. Spread on absorbent paper; cool.

Cream the cream cheese with ¼ cup butter or margarine. Add confectioners' sugar alternately with milk and vanilla. Beat until smooth. Add half the coconut. Spread on cake. Sprinkle with remaining coconut.

DUMP CAKE

1 pkg. Duncan Hines yellow cake
Mix
1 (20 oz.) can pineapple in syrup
(crushed), untrained

1 (21 oz.) can cherry pie filling
1 c. chopped pecans
½ c. butter (1 stick) or margarine,
cut in thin slices

Preheat oven to 350°. Grease 13 x 9 x 2-inch pan.

Dump undrained pineapple into pan; spread evenly. Dump in pie filling and spread into even layer. Dump dry cake mix onto cherry layer; spread evenly. Sprinkle pecans over cake mix. Put butter over top. Bake at 350° for 48 to 53 minutes. Serve warm.

LEMON CUSTARD CAKE

1 prepared angel food cake
(10-inch)
1 (3.4 oz) pkg. Instant lemon
Pudding mix

1 ½ c. cold milk
1 c. (8 oz.) sour cream
1 (21 oz.) can cherry or
strawberry pie filling

Tear the angel food cake into bite size pieces. Place in a 13 x 9 x 2-inch pan.

In a mixing bowl, combine the pudding mix, milk and sour cream; beat until thickened, about 2 minutes. Spread over cake. Spoon pie filling on top. Chill until serving time.

HOT FUDGE SUNDAE CAKE

1 c. all-purpose flour
1 c. chopped walnuts
3/4 c. sugar
2 Tbsp. cocoa
2 tsp. baking powder

½ c. milk
2 Tbsp. oil
1 tsp. vanilla
1 c. packed brown sugar
1 ¾ c. hot water

Preheat oven to 350°. Combine flour, walnuts, sugar, 2 tablespoons cocoa, baking powder, salt, milk, oil and vanilla until smooth. Pour into 9-inch round cake pan. Combine brown sugar and remaining cocoa; sprinkle over batter. Pour hot water over mixture.

Bake 40 minutes or until toothpick in center comes out clean. Serve with vanilla ice cream.

CALIFORNIA POUND CAKE

1 lb. (4 c.) powdered sugar

1 ½ c. (3 stick) butter

6 eggs

3 c, sifted cake flour

1 ½ tsp. vanilla

¼ tsp. salt

Cream together sugar and butter. Add eggs, one at a time, beating well after each addition. Blend in flour. Add vanilla and salt.

Pour into greased and floured 10-inch tube pan. Bake in a 350° oven for 60 to 65 minutes. Cool in pan for 5 minutes. Remove from pan and cool on rack.

LADY BALTIMORE CAKE

2 ¼ c. cake flour

1 ½ tsp. baking powder

½ tsp. salt

½ c. butter

1 1/3 c. sugar

1 tsp. vanilla

2/3 c. milk

4 egg whites

Sift flour with baking powder and salt. Cream butter thoroughly. Add sugar slowly and continue creaming until smooth and fluffy. Stir in vanilla. Add sifted dry ingredients alternately with milk in 4 or 5 portions, beginning and ending with flour and beating thoroughly after each addition. Fold in stiffly beaten egg whites.

Turn batter into two 8-inch layer cake pans. Bake at 375° for about 25 minutes or until cake is springy when lightly pressed with fingertips. Allow to cool in pans 5 minutes, then turn out onto cake racks and cool thoroughly.

MARASCHINO CHERRY CAKE

2 ½ c. cake flour
3 tsp. baking powder
¾ tsp. salt
½ c. butter
¾ c. sugar

2 eggs
1/3 c. maraschino cherry juice
2/3 c. milk
¾ c. sliced maraschino cherries

Sift flour with baking powder and salt. Cream butter until fluffy. Add sugar gradually and blend until smooth and creamy. Add eggs, one at a time, beating after each addition. Add flour mixture and liquids alternately, beginning and ending with flour. Mix well after each addition. Stir in cherries.

Pour into two greased and floured 8-inch layer cake pans. Bake at 350° for 30 minutes or until cake tests done. Place on rack to cool.

Remove from pans after 5 minutes. Frost with 7-Minute Frosting and decorate with maraschino cherry halves.

QUICK MIX MARBLE CAKE

2 c. all-purpose flour
3 ½ tsp baking powder
1 tsp. salt
1 (1 oz.) sq. unsweetened
Chocolate, melted
1 ¼ c. granulated sugar

½ c. butter
2 Tbsp. hot water
1 c. milk
1 tsp. vanilla
2 eggs
½ tsp. baking soda

In large bowl, sift flour with baking powder, salt and sugar. Add butter, milk and vanilla and stir with spoon for 2 minutes. Add eggs and beat for two more minutes. Pour 2/3 of this batter into an 8 x 12-inch greased and floured pan

Add cooled chocolate to the remaining batter. Then add the soda, dissolved in the water. Beat for ½ minute. Run chocolate batter over the light batter and cut a knife through several times for marble effect.

Bake in moderate oven at 350° for 35 to 40 minutes or until cake tests done. Cool on rack 15 minutes before removing from pan. Then cool thoroughly before frosting with Creamy Chocolate Frosting.

NUTMEG CAKE

¾ c. butter

2 c. sugar

4 eggs

3 c. all-purpose flour

2 tsp. nutmeg

1 ½ tsp. baking soda

¾ tsp. salt

1 ½ c. buttermilk

1 tsp. vanilla

1 ½ tsp. baking powder

Cream butter and sugar until light and fluffy. Add eggs, one at a time, beating well after each addition. Sift together dry ingredients. Add to creamed mixture alternately with buttermilk, beginning and ending with flour and beating well after each addition. Stir in vanilla.

Pour into 3 greased and floured 9-inch round cake pans. Bake at 350° for 25 to 30 minutes or until cakes teas done. Cool in pans on rack 10 minutes. Turn out of pans onto rack and cool completely. Frost.

Frosting:

3 egg whites

2 ½ c. sugar

2 ¼ tsp. light corn syrup

½ c. cold water

½ tsp. cream of tartar

dash of salt

1 ½ tsp. white vanilla flavoring

1 c. finely chopped walnuts

yellow food coloring (if desired)

Place egg whites and next 5 ingredients in top of double boiler (not overheat). Beat one minute with electric mixer to blend. Place over boiling water and cook, beating constantly, until frosting forms soft peaks, about 7 minutes. Remove from boiling water. Add vanilla and beat until frosting forms stiff peaks. Remove 2 cups of frosting to a separate bowl. Add walnuts to this mixture; mix well.

Spread between layers of cake. Tint the remaining frosting yellow, if desired. Frost top and sides of cake.

OLD-FASHIONED POUND CAKE

4 1/2 c. cake flour

1 ½ tsp. salt

½ tsp. mace

2 c. butter

2 ¼ c. granulated sugar

1 ½ tsp. vanilla

10 eggs, slightly beaten

Sift flour with salt and mace. Beat butter until creamy. Add sugar gradually and continue beating until smooth and fluffy. Add vanilla, then eggs in 4 or 5 portions, thoroughly beating after each portion. Add flour, ½ cup at a time, and mix well after each addition.

Turn batter into greased and floured tube pan. Bake at 350° for 1 hour. Remove from oven and cool for 5 minutes. Remove cake from pan to finish cooling

HALF-A-POUND CAKE

2 ¼ c. sifted cake flour

1 tsp. baking powder

¼ tsp. salt

¼ tsp. nutmeg

½ lb. butter

4 eggs

2 tsp. rose water

1 c. sugar

Combine flour, baking powder, salt and nutmeg. Cream butter thoroughly and add the flour mixture in 3 portions, mixing until smooth after each addition. Beat eggs until thick and lemon colored. Add flavoring and sugar all at once and beat until very light. Then beat the egg mixture thoroughly into the fat-flour mixture.

Pour into well-greased loaf pan. Bake in 350° oven for 1 ½ hours. Cool 5 minutes in pan before turning out onto wire cake rack to finish cooling. Makes 1 loaf.

BANANA CRUNCH CAKE

½ c. all-purpose flour

1 c. coconut

1 c. rolled oats

¾ c. firmly packed brown sugar

½ c. chopped pecans

½ c. margarine or butter

1 ½ c. (2 large) sliced very ripe bananas

½ c. dairy sour cream

4 eggs

1 pkg. Pillsbury Plus yellow cake mix

In medium bowl, combine flour, coconut, rolled oats, brown sugar and pecans; mix well. Using a fork, cut in margarine until mixture is crumbly; set aside. In large bowl, combine

Bananas, sour cream and eggs; blend until smooth. Add cake mix. Beat 2 minutes at high speed.

Spread 1/3 of batter in greased and floured tube pan. Sprinkle with 1/3 of coconut mixture. Repeat layers twice more, using remaining batter and coconut mixture, ending with coconut mixture.

Bake at 350° for 50 to 60 minutes or until toothpick inserted near center comes out clean. Cool upright in pan 15 minutes; remove from pan. Place on serving plate, coconut side up. Cool completely. Yields q6 servings.

SOCK-IT-TO-ME CAKE

1 pkg. Duncan Hines Butter Golden cake mix

1 c. (8 oz.) dairy sour cream

½ c. Crisco oil

4 eggs

¼ c. sugar

¼ c. water

Filling:

1 c. chopped pecans

2 Tbsp brown sugar

2 tsp. cinnamon

Preheat oven to 375°. In large bowl, blend cake mix sour cream, oil, ¼ cup sugar, water and eggs. Beat at high speed for 2 minutes. Pour 2/3 of the batter in a greased and floured 10-inch tube pan Spread remaining batter evenly over filling mixture.

Bake at 375° for 45 to 55minutes, until cack springs back when touched lightly. Cool right side up, for about 25 minutes, then remove from pan.

Glaze: Blend 1 cup confectioners' sugar and 2 tablespoons milk. Drizzle over cake.

CHOCOLATE MAYONNAISE CAKE

3 c. flour

1 ½ c. sugar

1/3 c cocoa

2 1/4tsp. baking powder

1 ½ tsp. baking soda

1 ½ cc. mayonnaise

1 ½ c. water

1 ½ tsp. vanilla

Grease two 9-inch layer pans. Line bottoms with wax paper.

Sift together dry ingredients into large bowl. Stir in mayonnaise. Gradually stir in water and vanilla until smooth and blended.

Pour into prepared pans. Bake in 350° oven for about 35 minutes. or until cake springs back when touched. Cool. Remove from pans. Makes 2 layers.

CARAMEL DREAM CAKE

1 BOX German chocolate cake mx

1 can Eagle brand condensed milk

1 c. Mrs. Richardson's butterscotch caramel topping

1 carton cool whip

2 crushed heath bars

Prepare cake mix according to package directions, Bake in 9 x 13-inch pan for 30 to 35 minutes. Remove from oven and let sit for five minutes.

Poke holes in cake with wooden spoon 1 inch apart, pour condensed milk and caramel topping into holes while cake is still hot. Cool. Refrigerate until ready to serve. Top with Cool Whip and garnish with crushed Heath bars.

7-UP POUND CAKE

3 STICKS BUTTER

3 c. sugar

3 c. sifted flour

¾ C. 7-Up

5 eggs, separated

1 ½ Tbsp. butter flavor extract

Cream butter and sugar for 20 minutes, Add flour alternately with 7-Up. Beat well. Add egg yolk, one at a time, beating well Add extract. Beat egg whites until stiff and fold in.

Pour into greased and floured Bundt pan. Bake in preheated oven at 350° for 1 hour and 10 minutes or until cake separates from pan.

GERMAN SEEET CHOCOLATE CAKE

1 (4 OZ) PKG. Bakers German's
Sweet chocolate

½ c. boiling water

2 stick butter or margarine

2 c. sugar

4 eggs, separated

1 tsp. vanilla

2 c. all-purpose flour

1 tsp. baking soda

1 tsp. salt

1 c. buttermilk

Melt chocolate in water; cool. Cream butter and sugar, Beat in egg yolks. Stir in vanilla and chocolate. Mix flour, soda and salt. Beat in flour mixture alternately with buttermilk. Beat egg whites until stiff peaks form, fold into batter.

Pour batter into three 9-inch layer pans, lined on bottoms with waxed paper. Bake at 350° for 30 minutes or until cake springs back when lightly pressed in center.

Cool 15 minutes. Remove from pan and column rack. Frost with Coconut-Pecan Frosting.

Coconut- Pecan Frosting:

1 ½ cans (12 oz.) evaporated milk

1 ½ c. sugar

4 slightly beaten egg yolks

¾ c. butter or margarine

1 ½ tap. Vanilla

2 c. flaked coconut

1 ½ c. chopped pecans

Combine milk, sugar, egg yolks, butter or margarine and vanilla in saucepan. Cook and stir over medium heat until thickened.

Remove from heat. Stir in coconut and pecans. Cool until thick enough to spread. Makes 4 ¼ cups.

SPECIAL BIRTHDAY CAKE

1 BOX Duncan Hines Butter
Yellow cake mix
¼ tsp. baking powder
3 Tbsp. sugar

¼ c. butter
4 eggs
1 (11 oz.) can drained mandarin
oranges

Combine all ingredients, except oranges. Beat at high speed until light and fluffy. Fold in oranges. Bake cake as directed at 350° in three 8-inch round cake pans.

Frosting:

1 (16 oz.) container Cool Whip
1 (6 oz.) box vanilla instant pudding mix

1 (20 oz.) can pineapple and juice

Combine all ingredients and mix well. Frost cooled cake.

POUND CAKE

1 LB. POWDERED SUGAR
1 LB. BUTTER

6 EGGS
1 LB. CAKE FLOUR (DON'T PACK)

Cream sugar and butter until fluffy. Beat the eggs together until they are beaten well; add to the sugar and butter. Add the flour and mix well.

Bake in greased and floured tube pan at 300° for 45 minutes. Then bake at 325° for 30 minutes or until done.

SCRIPTURE CAKE

2 ½ c. 2 Samuel 13.8
5 tsp. Galatians 5.9
½ tsp. Mark 9.50
¾ tsp. 1 Kings 10.10
3 Tbsp. Proverbs 30.33

¾ c. Jeremiah 6.20
1 c. Isaiah 10.14
¾ c. 1 Corinthians 3.2
½ c. Proverbs 25.11
½ c. 1 Samuel 30.12

Follow Numbers 11.8. Preheat oven to 350°. Sift dry ingredients.
Cream butter and sugar. Add eggs. Add dry ingredients alternately with milk. Mix in apples and raisins by hand.
Pour into greased loaf pan. Bake about 45 minutes until golden brown. Test with toothpick.

91

APPLESAUCE SPICE CAKE

½ C. oil

¾ C. honey

1 1/3 C. applesauce

¼ stick butter

1 tsp. vanilla

2 c. all-purpose flour

1 tsp. baking powder

2 ½ tsp. cinnamon

½ tsp. ground cloves

1/4 tsp. ginger

1/8 tsp. allspice

¼ tsp. nutmeg

Preheat oven to 350°. In large bowl, blend the oil, honey, and applesauce. Cut butter into small squares and heat it in a medium-sized saucepan over low heat until the butter is melted. Add the oil-honey-applesauce mixture and stir until smooth. Add vanilla and stir. Remove from heat and return to mixing bowl. Add the flour, baking powder and spices, blending well. Batter will be a little sticky.

Pour batter into a greased and floured 8-inch square pan. Bake in a preheated oven for 30 to 40 minutes. Cool and top with Apple-sauce syrup.

Applesauce Syrup:

3 Tbsp. butter

3 Tbsp. berry jam or preserves

2 Tbsp. honey

1 small apple, peeled, cored and grated

Place all ingredients in a saucepan. Boil 3 to 4 minutes. Serve hot on cake.

BEST MOLASSES CAKE

½ c. shortening

1 ¼ c. molasses

½ tsp. salt

1 egg, beaten

2 c. all-purpose flour

1 tsp. baking powder

1 tsp. cinnamon

½ tsp. nutmeg

¾ c. boiling water

1 ½ tsp. soda

3 Tbsp. cocoa

½ tsp. vanilla

Mix shortening, molasses, salt and egg, then stir in flour, baking powder and spices. Last, add hot water, mixed with soda, cocoa and vanilla. Bake in 375° oven about 30 minutes in tube pan.

LEMON CUSTARD PUDDING CAKE

6 Tbsp. all-purpose flour

6 Tbsp. butter, melted

2 c. sugar, divided

4 eggs, separated

1 ½ c. milk

grated peel of 1 lemon

2 Tbsp. lemon juice

confectioners' sugar

In a large mixing bowl, combine flour, butter and 1 ½ cups sugar. Beat egg yolks; add to mixing bowl along with milk and lemon peel. Mix well. Add lemon juice.

In another bowl, beat egg whites until stiff, slowly adding remaining ½ cup sugar while beating. Fold into batter.

Pour into a greased 2-quart baking dish and place in shallow pan of hot water. Bake at 350° for 55 to 60 minutes or until lightly browned. Serve warm or chilled with confectioners sugar dusted on top.

HOT MILK CAKE

4 eggs

2 c. sugar

2 ¼ c. all-purpose flour

2 ¼ tsp. baking powder

1 tsp. vanilla

1 ¼ c. milk

10 Tbsp. butter

In mixing bowl, beat eggs at high speed until thick, about 5 minutes. Gradually add sugar, beating until mixture is lightly and fluffy. Combine flour and baking powder. Add to batter with vanilla and beat at low speed until smooth.

In saucepan, heat milk and butter just until butter melts, stirring occasionally. Add to batter, beating until combined.

Pour into greased 13 x 9 x 2-inch baking pan. Bake at 350° for 30 to 35 minutes or until cake tests done. Cool on a wire rack.

LUSCIOUS COCONUT CAKE

Cake:

2 sticks butter, softened

2 c. sugar

5 eggs

3 c. all-purpose flour

1 Tbsp. baking powder

1 ¼ c. milk

1 tsp. vanilla

7-Minute Frosting

2 egg whites

1 ½ c. sugar

1/8 tsp. salt

½ c. water

1 Tbsp. light corn syrup

½ tsp. vanilla

½ tsp. lemon extract

1 ½ C. shredded coconut

Preheat oven to 350°. Grease and flour three 9-inch round layer cake pans.

Cake: beat butter until creamy. Gradually add sugar, beating thoroughly. Add eggs, one at a time, beating well after each addition. Combine flour and baking powder in small bowl. Add to batter alternately with milk, mixing thoroughly. Beat in vanilla. Divide batter equally among prepared pans.

Bake in 350° oven for 25 minutes or until a toothpick inserted in center comes out clean. Cool cakes in pans on wire racks.

Frosting: Combine egg whites, sugar, salt, water and corn syrup in heavy saucepan. Heat over low heat, beating constantly with hand mixer and scraping down sides to prevent sugar crystals, until soft peaks form, about 7 minutes. Don't overbeat. Remove from heat. Add vanilla and lemon; beat 1 minute.

POTATO CAKE

1 c. butter, softened

2 c. sugar

2 eggs

1 c. cold mashed potatoes

1 tsp. vanilla

2 c. all-purpose flour

¼ c. baking soda

1 tsp. baking soda

1 c. milk

1 c. chopped nuts

In a mixing bowl, cream butter and sugar until fluffy. Add eggs, one at a time, beating well after each addition. Blend in potatoes and vanilla. Combine flour, cocoa and baking soda. Add alternately with milk, blending well after each addition. Stir in nuts.

Pour into greased 13 x 9 x 2-inch baking pan. Bake at 350° for 40 to 45 minutes or until cake tests done. Cool on a wire rack.

EASY-CHEESY LEMON BARS

Base:

1 pkg. Pillsbury Plus lemon cake mix

1/3 c. margarine or butter, softned

1 egg

Topping:

1 can Pillsbury's ready-to-spread Lemon
    Frosting Supreme

1 egg

8 oz. pkg. cream cheese, softened

½ c. chopped pecans

Heat oven to 350°. Grease and flour 13 x 9-inch pan.

Base: in a large bowl, combine cake mix, margarine and egg at low speed until crumbly. Press in prepared pan.

Topping: in a small bowl combine frosting, cream cheese and egg and low speed until well blended. Beat at highest speed until smooth. Stir in nuts. Spread over base.

Bake at 350° for 40 to 50 minutes or until firm to the touch. Cool completely. Yields 36 bars.

WALNUT FROSTIES

1 c. firmly packed brown sugar

1 ¾ all-purpose flour

½ c. butter, softened

½ tsp. soda

1 tsp. vanilla

¼ tsp. salt

1 egg

Topping:

1 c. chopped walnuts

¼ c. dairy sour cream

½ c. firmly packed brown sugar

Heat oven to 350°. In large bowl cream brown sugar and margarine until light and fluffy. Blend in vanilla and egg. Lightly spoon flour into measuring cup; level off. Gradually add flour, soda and salt to creamed mixture; mix well.

Shape dough into 1-inch balls. Place 2 inches apart on ungreased cookie sheets. With thumb, make imprint in center of each cookie. Combine topping ingredients. Fill each cookie with 1 teaspoon topping.

Bake at 350° for 10 to 14 minutes or until delicately browned. Makes 3 dozen cookies.

MOM'S SOFT RAISIN COOKIES

1 c. water

2 c. raisins

1 c. shortening

1 ¼ c. sugar

2 eggs, slightly beaten

1 tsp. vanilla

3 ½ c. all-purpose flour

1 tsp. baking powder

1 tsp. baking soda

1 tsp. salt

½ tsp. cinnamon

½ tsp. nutmeg

½ tsp. chopped walnuts

Combine raisins and water in a small saucepan; bring to boil. Cook for 3 minutes. Remove from heat and let cool. Do not drain.

In a mixing bowl, cream shortening. Gradually add sugar. Add eggs and vanilla. Combine dry ingredients; gradually add to creamed mixture and blend thoroughly. Stir in nuts and raisins.

Drop by teaspoonfuls 2 inches apart on ungreased baking sheets. Bake at 350° for 12 to 14 minutes. Makes about 6 dozen.

Note: drain raisins just before adding to mixture.

ALMOND ROCA

1 c. crushed almonds

12 Hershey bars

1 c. butter

1 c. sugar

Line 8 x 8-inch pan with almonds, then 6 Hershey bars. Break to fit.

Boil butter and sugar until golden brown, stirring constantly. Pour hot mixture on chocolate. Place remaining bars on top and sprinkle with almonds. Break or cut while still warm.

COW PIES

2 c. (12 oz.) milk chocolate chips

1 Tbsp. shortening

½ c. raisins

½ c. chopped, silvered almonds

In double boiler, over simmering water, melt the chocolate chips and shortening, stirring until smooth. Remove from the heat. Stir in raisins and almonds.

Drop by tablespoonfuls onto waxed paper. Chill until ready to serve. Makes 2 dozen.

DIVINITY

1 c. sugar	2/3 c. light corn syrup
½ c. water	¼ tsp. salt
1/8 tsp. cream of tartar	¼ c. water
3 egg white	1 tsp. vanilla
2 c. sugar	1 c. pecans

Put the 1 cup sugar, ½ cup water and cream of tartar into saucepan; stir to blend. Then boil rapidly, without stirring to 240° (medium ball) or until syrup will spin a thread 6 inches long when dropped from a fork. Immediately remove from heat. Meanwhile, beat egg whites until stiff.

In another saucepan, have combined the 2 cups sugar, corn syrup, salt and ¼ cup water. When the first mixture is done, place the second mixture over the heat and boil, with occasionally stirring, until syrup reached 280° (medium crack stage).

Pour the first syrup, while still hot, over beaten whites, adding slowly and beating continuously until stiff and smooth. Set aside until second syrup is done. Cool a minute or two, then pour it slowly over first mixture, continuing to beat until smooth and so stiff that it is hard to handle. Stir in flavoring and nuts.

Turn into buttered pan and press out smooth. When set, cut into squares. Makes about 2 pounds.

Candied fruits, such as cherries and pineapple, may be cut fine and folded in with the nuts for attractive color.

SEAFOAM

2 c. granulated sugar	1 tsp. vanilla
½ c. corn syrup	½ c. cut candied cherries
½ c. water	½ c. broken walnut pieces
2 egg whites	

Boil sugar, corn syrup and water until mixture forms a hard ball in cold water (250°). Have egg whites beaten until stiff and add syrup slowly, beating constantly. When stiff, fold in vanilla, cherries and nuts.

Drop from tip of spoon onto waxed paper. Cool before removing from paper and serving. Makes about 1 pound.

5-MINUTE FUDGE

3 c. sugar

¾ c. butter

1 (5 ½ oz.) can evaporated milk

1 (12 oz.) pkg, semi-sweet chocolate pieces

1 (7 oz.) jar kraft Marshmallow Crème

1 tsp. vanilla

1 c. chopped nuts

Combine sugar, butter and milk in heavy 2-quart saucepan. Bring to full rolling boil, stirring constantly. Continue boiling for 5 minutes over medium heat or at 234° on candy thermometer, stirring constantly, to prevent scorching.

Remove from heat. Stir in chocolate pieces until melted. Add Marshmallow Crème, nuts and vanilla. Beat until well blended.

Pour into greased 13 x 9-inch pan. Cool at room temperature. Cut into squares. Makes 3 pounds.

MARVELOUS MARBLE FUDGE

½ c. Karo light corn syrup

1/3 c. evaporated milk

2 (8 oz. each) pkg. Baker's semi-sweet chocolate

1/3 c. peanut butter

2 tsp. vanilla

¾ c. Confectioners' sugar

Line 8 x 8 x 2-inch pan with plastic wrap.

In 2-quart saucepan, stir corn syrup and milk. Add chocolate. Stirring constantly, cook over medium-low heat until chocolate is melted. Remove from heat. Stir in vanilla. Add sugar. With wooden spoon, beat until smooth.

Spread in pan. Drop peanut butter by teaspoonfuls on fudge. With knife, swirl peanut butter through fudge to marbleize. Chill 2 hours or until firm.

Invert onto cutting board. Peel off plastic wrap. Cut with sharp knife. Makes about 25 (1 ½ inch) squares.

MASHED POTATO FUDGE

1 medium (1/2 c.) unseasoned cooked, mashed potato

3 c. powdered sugar

1 c. flaked or shredded coconut

1 tsp. vanilla

2 sq. semi-sweet chocolate

While the potato is hot, beat in the sugar and coconut, then the vanilla. Press into a lightly greased 8-inch square pan. Melt chocolate and pour over top. Chill and cut into squares. Keep indefinitely in airtight container in refrigerator. Makes 64 (1-inch) pieces.

Alternate: omit chocolate from recipe above. Combine mashed potato, sugar, coconut and vanilla in mixing bowl and cream thoroughly. Chill several hours.

Remove and turn onto damp surfaces. Knead with hands until mixture is creamy. Shape into 1-inch balls. Place in candy papers and serve. Store in airtight container for about two weeks.

NUTTY CHRISTMAS CREAMS

½ c. butter or margarine, softened

1 (14 oz.) can sweetened condensed milk

1 Tbsp. vanilla extract

2 (16 oz.) pkg. sifted powdered sugar

4 c. chopped pecans

2 c. mixed, candied fruit

Combine butter, milk and vanilla in a large mixing bowl. Beat at medium speed until blended. Gradually add powdered sugar, beating well after each addition. Stir in pecans and candied fruit.

Spoon into buttered 13 x 9 x 2-inch baking pan. Cover and chill overnight. Cut into squares. Store in refrigerator. Yields 4 ½ pounds.

COCONUT-CHOCOLATE DIPPED CANDIES

2 lb. powdered sugar

2 lb. fine coconut

1 c. finely chopped walnuts

1 small can evaporated milk

1 pkg. chocolate chips

½ bar paraffin wax

In large bowl, mix powdered sugar, coconut and walnuts. Add evaporated milk and mix well. Roll into balls. Place on cookie sheet on waxed paper. Cover with foil and refrigerate until following day.

Over double boiler, melt chocolate chips and paraffin wax. Keep chocolate warm over hot water. Dip balls, 2 or 3 at a time, into chocolate, coating evenly. Lift out on tine of fork. Let excess drip off. Cool on waxed paper.

These keep well in refrigerator and also freeze well. Makes 200 to 250.

CHERRY DELIGHTS

1 c. margarine
½ c. sugar
½ c. light corn syrup
2 eggs, separated

2 ½ c. flour
2 c. finely chopped nuts
candied cherry halves

Mix margarine and sugar. Stir in corn syrup, egg yolks and flour. Chill.

Roll into 1-inch balls. Dip into slightly beaten egg whites, then nuts. Place on greased cookie sheet. Press cherry into center of each cookie. Bake 325° for 20 minutes. Makes 4 dozen.

ORANGE COCONUT CREAMS

1 Tbsp. butter
2 c. granulated sugar
¼ c. water
½ c. evaporated milk

2 tsp. orange-flavored water
2 tsp. orange juice
¼ tsp. grated orange rind
2 c. moist, shredded coconut

Melt butter in pan in which candy is to be cooked. Add sugar, water and milk and boil to soft ball stage (236°), stirring constantly. Cool and beat vigorously for 2 minutes. Add flavoring, rind and coconut and knead into candy until creamy.

Using about a tablespoon of candy, mold with the hands into even-sized balls. Roll in additional coconut. Makes 1 ½ pounds.

PEANUT BUTTER BALLS

2 lb. peanut butter
1 lb. butter

3 (1 lb.) powdered sugar

Mix all ingredients well and shape into balls. Chill.

Melt ¾ stick paraffin wax in top of double boiler. Add 3 large bags chocolate chips; stir until melted.

Insert toothpick in end of ball. Dip into mixture and drain on waxed paper. Chill until chocolate is set.

PEANUT BRITTLE

2 c. raw Spanish peanuts
1 c. white karo syrup
1 c. sugar

1 Tbsp. butter
1 tsp. baking soda

Combine peanuts, syrup and sugar in large pan. Bring to a boil. Boil, stirring constantly, until golden brown, about 10 minutes. Remove from heat. Add butter and baking soda. Stir quickly and pour onto a greased cookie sheet. Let cool. Break into pieces.

PEANUT BUTTER FUDGE

2 ½ c. sugar
1 2/3 c. milk
20 oz. jar chunky peanut butter

7 ½ oz. jar Marshmallow crème
½ tsp. vanilla

Combine sugar and milk in saucepan. Cook over low heat to soft ball stage. Turn off heat. Add peanut butter, Marshmallow crème and vanilla. Mix quickly and pour into foil-lined pan. Let cool and cut into squares.

CANDIED WALNUTS

1 c. brown sugar
½ c. granulated sugar
½ c. sour cream

dash of salt
1 tsp. vanilla
2 ½ c. walnut halves

Combine brown sugar, granulated sugar and sour cream in a small saucepan. Cook over medium heat, stirring until it boils. Continue to boil until mixture reaches soft ball stage (240°) or until it forms a soft ball when dropped into cold water. Stir in salt and vanilla.

Pour hot candy mixture over walnuts in a mixing bowl. Mix until walnuts are evenly coated. Spoon out onto waxed paper. Separate walnuts. Allow to cool and set. When dry, store in airtight container.

WALNUT-BUTTERSCOTCH FUDGE

2/3 c. evaporated milk

1 (7 oz.) jar Marshmallow Crème

1 c. granulated sugar

½ stick butter or margarine

1 (12oz) bag butterscotch chips

1 ¼ tsp. vanilla extract

1 c. walnuts, chopped

Line an 8-inch square pan with foil, letting ends extend above pan on 2 sides.

Put evaporated milk, Marshmallow Crème, sugar and butter in a medium-sized saucepan. Stirring constantly to prevent scorching, bring to boil. Reduce heat and boil 5 minutes.

Remove from heat. Stir in chips until melted. Stir in vanilla and walnuts until blended. Pour into lined pan. Chill 2 hours or until firm.

Lift foil by ends onto cutting board. Cut into squares. Store in refrigerator. Makes 64 pieces.

DESSERT IN A GLASS

2 (8 oz.) cartoons lemon yogurt

1 (15 ½ oz.) can crushed pineapple

1 c. milk

1 c. ice cubes

2 Tbsp. sugar

mint sprigs

In a blender container, combine yogurt, undrained pineapple and milk. Cover and blend until mixture is smooth. With blender running, add ice cubes, one at a time, through hole in lid, until slushy. Sweeten to taste with sugar. Chill until serving time.

Pour into glasses. To serve, garnish with fresh mint, if desired. Makes 6 servings.

OLD FASHIONED VANILLA ICE CREAM

1 ½ tsp. cornstarch

¼ tsp. salt

¾ c. sugar

3 c. whole milk

2 eggs, beaten

2 c. whipping cream

1 ½ tsp. vanilla

Mix cornstarch, salt and sugar in top of double boiler to a thin, smooth paste with 2 cups of the milk. Cook over boiling water for 20 minutes with occasionally stirring.

Beat eggs until light. Gradually stir in a small amount of the hot cornstarch mixture and return to double boiler to 2 cook 2 minutes longer with constant stirring. Cool.

Pour through strainer. Stir in rest of milk, cream and vanilla. Pour into freezer can and freeze according to directions.

PINEAPPLE BUTTERMILK SHERBET

1 qt. fresh buttermilk

9 oz. can crushed pineapple

1 tsp. lemon juice

1/8 tsp. salt

1 c. sugar

2 egg whites, stiffly beaten

Mix together all ingredients, except egg whites and pour into freezing tray of refrigerator. Set refrigerator at coldest temperature and freeze until mushy.

Pour into chilled bowl and beat until smooth with rotary beater. Fold in stiffly beaten egg whites thoroughly. Immediately return to chilled trays and continue freeze until firm.

FRESH PEACH COBBLER

Pastry for deep dish pie

2 ½ lb. ripe, juicy peaches (about 4 c. sliced)

¾ c. sugar

4 drops almond extract

1 tsp. vanilla

¼ tsp. cinnamon

¼ tsp. nutmeg

2 Tbsp. butter

Roll pastry to fit inside of 6-cup baking dish or casserole. Bring pastry up around sides of dish and overlap slightly.

In mixing bowl, mix peaches, sugar, extracts and spices. Pour into casserole. Dot with butter and cover with remaining pastry; trim. Turn under and flute edge.

Bake in a hot oven (450°) for 15 minutes. Then reduce to 325° and bake 10 to 15 minutes longer or until crust is golden brown. Serve warm.

RAISIN COBBLER

Pastry:

 1 c. all-purpose flour
 ½ tsp. salt

1/3 c. shortening
3 Tbsp. ice water

Filling:

 2/3 c. sugar
 2 Tbsp. cornstarch
 2/3 c. orange juice
 2/3 c. water
 2 c. seedless raisins

1 Tbsp. butter
1 tsp. lemon juice
¼ tsp. salt
1 small seedless orange, sliced

Combine flour, salt and shortening. Add ice water; mix well. Pat or roll out dough to ¼-inch thickness and fit in bottom and around sides of deep-dish pie pan.

Blend sugar and cornstarch in saucepan. Stir in next 3 ingredients. Cook, with constant stirring, until liquid is just clear and thickened.

Remove from heat. Stir in butter, lemon juice and salt, then fold in orange slices. Turn into prepared pie pan. Bake in 425° oven for 30 minutes or until crust is golden brown. Serve warm.

GLORIFIED RICE

1 (14 oz.) box Minute rice
1 (20 oz.) can crushed pineapple, drained
2 tsp. vanilla

1 c. mini marshmallows
1 (8 oz.) cool whip
½ small jar maraschino cherries, sliced 1 c. sugar

Cook rice; cool completely. Add remaining ingredients. Use some cherries for garnishing top.

QUICK CHERRY DESSERT

2 sticks butter or margarine

1 ½ granulated sugar

4 eggs

1 tsp. almond extract

2 c. all-purpose flour

2 tsp. baking powder

1 (21 oz.) can cherry pie filling

powdered sugar to dust over top

(optional)

In large mixing bowl, cream together the butter and sugar. Add the eggs. Beat until light and fluffy. Add the almond extract. Stir in the flour and baking powder. Mix until smooth.

Butter a 13 x 9-inch cake pan. Turn the mixture into the pan. Spoon the pie filling onto the cake in 16 spots, spacing 4 spoonful's evenly in each direction.

Bake at 350° for 45 to 50 minutes or until golden and cake tests done. Filling will sink into the cake while baking.

To serve, cut into 16 pieces. Place, bottom side up, on serving plate. Dust with powdered sugar, if spoon used. Spoon slightly sweetened whipped cream over each serving. This is great warm!

PINEAPPLE BAKE

8 slices day-old bread, cut into 1-inch cubes

1 (20 oz.) can crushed pineapple, drained

4 large eggs

½ c. unsalted butter, melted

¾ c. packed light brown sugar

Heat oven to 350°. Butter a 1 ½-quart baking dish. Toss bread and pineapple in medium size bowl. Spread out in baking dish.

In small bowl, beat eggs with electric mixer or wire whisk until light and fluffy. Beat in butter and sugar until blended. Pour over bread mixture.

Bake about 40 minutes, until puffed and golden. Serve immediately. Makes 6 servings.

COCONUT APRICOT BARS

2 eggs

½ c. brown sugar, packed

½ c. softened butter or margarine

½ c. water

1 pkg. lemon cake mix

1 c. flaked coconut

1 c. chopped, dried apricots

Beat eggs, sugar, butter, water and half the cake mix until smooth. Stir the remaining cake mix, coconut and apricots in.

Spread in greased and floured jelly roll pan, 15 ½ x 10 ½ x 1-inch. Bake at 375° for 20 to 25 minutes. Cool.

Spread with cream cheese frosting. Cut into 3 x 1 ½-inch bars. Makes 30 bars.

GRANNY'S PEANUT BUTTER COOKIES

1 c. butter or margarine

¾ c. brown sugar

¾ c. granulated sugar

1 tsp. vanilla

1 c. peanut butter (chunky)

2 eggs, beaten

1 ¼ c. all-purpose flour

1 c. bran

¾ c. rolled oats

2 tsp. baking soda

Melt butter. Beat together with the sugars, vanilla, peanut butter and eggs. In separate bowl, combine the flour, bran, oats and baking soda. Stir mixture into butter mixture.

Drop by teaspoons onto ungreased cookie sheet. Bake at 350° for 15 to 18 minutes. Remove to rack to cool.

MELTING MOMENTS

1 c. flour

½ c. confectioners' sugar

½ c. cornstarch

1 c. soft butter

1 can coconut

Sift flour, sugar and cornstarch. Blend in butter until soft dough is formed. Shape into small balls. Roll in coconut.

Place on ungreased baking sheets 1 ½ inches apart. Bake at 300° for 20 to 25 minutes or until lightly browned. Makes 3 to 3 ½ dozen.

QUICK CRISPY COOKIES

1 c. butter or margarine, softened

½ c. firmly packed brown sugar

1 ½ c. crushed corn flakes

1 ¾ c. all-purpose flour

½ tsp. ground cinnamon

¼ tsp. ground nutmeg

1/8 tsp. ground cloves

¼ tsp. ground allspice

¼ tsp. ground nutmeg

1 c. finely chopped pecans

1 ½ tsp. vanilla extract

powdered sugar

Cream butter at medium speed. Gradually add sugar, beating until light and fluffy. Combine flour and spices; add to creamed mixture well. Stir in corn flakes, pecans and vanilla.

Shape mixture into 1-inch balls and place 1 inch apart on greased cookie sheets. Bake at 350° for 15 to 20 minutes or until lightly browned.

Remove to wire racks and cool completely. Sprinkle with powdered sugar. Yields about 4 ½ dozen.

TEN MINUTE MAGIC MACAROONS

1 can sweetened condensed milk
3 to 4 c. shredded coconut

1 tsp. vanilla

Mix milk with coconut and vanilla. Drop by spoonsful onto greased cookie sheet. Bake in 350° oven until delicately brown. Remove from pan immediately.

PEANUT BUTTER KISSES

½ c. smooth peanut butter
½ c. margarine
½ c. white sugar
½ c. brown sugar
1 egg

1 tsp. vanilla
2 c. flour
½ tsp. soda
½ tsp. salt
1 (12 oz) bag Hershey's kisses

Cream together peanut butter, margarine, white sugar and brown sugar. Beat together egg and vanilla. Add flour sifted with soda and salt. Add to peanut butter mixture. Mix well. Make balls from 1 teaspoon of mixture. Roll each ball in white sugar.
Grease cookie sheet. Bake at 350° for 10 minutes only. Remove from oven and quickly press a Hershey's Kiss in center of each cookie. Return to oven for 3 minutes only.

BROWNIE DROPS

2 (4 oz.) pkg. sweet baking chocolate
1 Tbsp. butter
2 eggs
¾ c. sugar
¼ c. all-purpose flour

1/8 tsp. salt
¼ tsp. cinnamon
¼ tsp. baking powder
½ tsp. vanilla extract
walnut halves

Combine chocolate and butter in top of a double boiler. Cook over boiling water until chocolate melts, stirring occasionally. Cool and set aside.
Beat eggs at high speed until foamy. Gradually add sugar, beating until mixture is thick and lemon-colored, about 5 minutes. Add chocolate mixture and next 4 ingredients, mixing well. Stir in vanilla.
Drop by teaspoonfuls 3 inches apart on greased cookie sheets. Press a walnut into center of each cookie. Bake at 350° for 8 to 10 minutes. Cool on wire rack. Yields 5 dozen.

RAISIN BRAN JUMBLES

6 Tbsp. butter or margarine

½ c. brown sugar, packed

1 egg, beaten

½ c. Raisin Bran

1 c. all-purpose flour

½ c. oatmeal

½ tsp. baking powder

½ tsp. baking soda

1/3 c. raisins

¼ c. chopped walnuts

Cream butter and sugar; beat in egg. Combine Raisin Bran, flour, oatmeal, baking powder and baking soda; stir into butter mixture. Add raisins and walnuts.

Drop by tablespoons onto a greased cookie sheet. Bake at 375° for 12 minutes. Cool on rack.

MOIST PINEAPPLE COOKIES

2/3 c. butter or margarine

1 ¼ c. brown sugar, well packed

2 eggs

1 (15 ¼ oz.) can crushed pineapple (reserve juice)

1 tsp. vanilla

½ tsp. salt

2 ½ c. all-purpose flour

1 tsp. baking soda

1 tsp. baking powder

½ c. chopped nuts

thinly sliced candied pineapple (for garnish)

Glaze:

1 Tbsp. butter or margarine

1 ½ c. powdered sugar

3 to 4 tbsp. pineapple juice

Cream butter with brown sugar. Add eggs and beat until fluffy. Stir in the pineapple, soda, baking powder, vanilla and salt; mix well. Add the flour and blend well. Stir in nuts until evenly blended.

Drop by small spoonful's on greased baking sheet. Bake at 375° for 10 to 12 minutes or until golden around the edges.

Meanwhile, brown the butter for the glaze in a saucepan over medium heat. Stir in the powdered sugar and enough of the reserved pineapple juice to make a smooth glaze.

Cool cookies. Use a spoon to spread on the glaze. Top with thin slices of candied pineapple.

GERMAN CRACKER BAR COOKIE BARS

½ c. butter or margarine
1 pkg. German chocolate cake mix
3 c. miniature marshmallows
1 (6 oz.) pkg. butterscotch pieces

½ c. flaked coconut
1 c. chopped pecans
1 (14 oz.) can sweetened condensed milk

Preheat oven to 350°. In oven, melt butter in jelly roll pan, 15 ½ x 10 ½ x 1-inch. Rotate pan until butter covers bottom. Sprinkle cake mix (dry) in pan. Sprinkle cake mix (dry) in pan. Sprinkle marshmallows, butterscotch pieces, coconut and nuts over cake mix in order listed. Pour milk evenly over top.

Bake about 25 minutes or until golden brown. Run knife around edges to loosen sides. Cool. Cut into 3 x 2 ½ inch bars. Makes 30 bars.

HOLIDAY FRUIT COOKIES

2 eggs, beaten
¾ c. sugar
½ c. molasses
1 ½ tsp. soda
1 ½ Tbsp. water
½ tsp. cinnamon

½ tsp. nutmeg
½ tsp. cloves
¼ c. fruit juice
2 c. all-purpose flour
1 c. raisins
1 c. nuts

Beat the eggs; add sugar and molasses and mix well. Add soda, dissolved in water. Add spices, fruit juice and half the flour. Dredge raisins and nuts with the other half of the flour and add to the batter.

Drop by teaspoons onto a greased cookie sheet and bake at 350° for about 12 to 15 minutes. Makes 4 dozen.

CAKE MIX COOKIES

1 pkg. cake mix (any kind)
2 eggs

½ c. shortening
4 Tbsp. water

Mix all ingredients in a large bowl. Drop by teaspoons onto an ungreased cookie sheet. Bake for 10 minutes at 350°. Makes 3 dozen cookies.

TEXAS BROWNIES

2 c. all-purpose flour

2 c. granulated sugar

½ c. (1 stick) butter or margarine

½ c. shortening

1 c. strong brewed coffee

¼ c. dark unsweetened cocoa

½ c. buttermilk

2 eggs

1 tsp. baking soda

1 tsp. vanilla

Frosting:

½ c. (1 stick) butter or margarine

2 Tbsp. dark cocoa

¼ c. milk

3 ½ c. unsifted powdered sugar

1 tsp. vanilla

In large mixing bowl, combine the flour and the sugar. In heavy saucepan, combine butter, shortening, coffee and cocoa. Stir and heat to boiling. Pour boiling mixture over the flour and sugar in the bowl. Add the buttermilk, eggs, baking soda and vanilla. Mix well, using a wooden spoon or high speed on electric mixer.

Pour into a well-buttered 12 ½ x 11-inch jelly roll pan. Bake at 400° for 20 minutes or until Brownie's test done in the center. While brownies bake, prepare the frosting.

In a saucepan, combine the butter, cocoa and milk. Heat to boiling, stirring. Mix in the powdered sugar and vanilla until frosting is smooth.

Pour warm frosting over brownies as soon as you take them out of the oven. Cool. Cut into 48 bars.

CHUNKY CHOCOLATE COOKIE SQUARES

2 ½ c. all-purpose flour

1 tsp baking soda

½ tsp. salt

¾ c. butter (1 ½ sticks)

1 c. firmly packed brown sugar

¾ c. Karo light or dark corn syrup

1 egg

1 tsp. vanilla

1 c. chopped pecans

2 (4 oz. each) pkg. Baker's

German's sweet chocolate, cut

into large chunks

Mix flour, baking soda and salt; set aside. Beat butter and sugar in large bowl of electric mixer at medium speed until light and fluffy. Slowly beat in corn syrup, then egg and vanilla. Beat in flour mixture until blended. Stir in pecans and half the chocolate.

Spread evenly in ungreased 12 ½ x 10 ½ x 1-inch jelly roll pan. Sprinkle remaining chocolate on top. Bake at 350° for 30 minutes or until lightly brown. Cool on rack. Cut into 2 ½-inch squares. Makes 2 dozen.

CHOCOLATE SYRUP BROWNIES

½ c. butter or margarine

1 c. sugar

3 eggs

1 c. all-purpose flour

¾ c. canned chocolate-flavored syrup

1 tsp. vanilla extract

1 c. chopped walnuts

Cream together butter, sugar and eggs until well blended. Stir in flour, chocolate syrup, vanilla and nuts. Turn into greased and lightly floured 9-inch square pan.

Bake at 350° for 40 minutes or until tester inserted near center comes out clean. Cool in pan on wire rack. Cut into 16 squares. Remove from pan and store in airtight container.

CHOCOLATE CHIP COOKIES

1 c. butter

1 c. granulated sugar

4 c. brown sugar

2 eggs

2 c. flour

1 tsp. soda

1 tsp. salt

2 c. old-fashioned oats

2 tsp. vanilla

1 (12 oz.) pkg. chocolate chips

Cream butter and sugars at medium speed for 2 minutes. Add eggs beating well. Sift and add flour, soda and salt. Stir in oats, vanilla and chocolate chips.

Drop by tablespoons onto ungreased cookie sheet. Bake 10 minutes at 350°.

EASY COOKIES

2 egg whites, stiffly beaten

¾ c. sugar

1 tsp. vanilla

1 c. chocolate chips

½ c. chopped walnuts

½ c. raisins

Preheat oven to 350°. Gradually add sugar to beaten egg whites. Add vanilla. Beat. Stir in chocolate chips, walnuts and raisins.

Grease cookie sheets with butter. Turn off oven. Drop 1/2 tea- spoon cookie batter onto cookie sheets about 1 inch apart. Place in oven. Leave in oven 45 to 60 minutes. Take cookies out. Cool. Makes approximately 60 cookies.

SWEET POTATO PUDDING

1 stick butter

4 c. grated raw sweet potatoes

1 c. molasses

½ c. sugar

1 tsp. allspice

1 tsp. cinnamon

1 c. milk

½ c. chopped nuts

1 c. raisins

½ tsp. cloves

3 eggs, beaten

In heavy, iron skillet, melt the butter. Mix all ingredients together, adding eggs last. Pour mixture in the hot pan of butter. Stir until heated.

Put skillet into 350° oven to bake. When crusted around edge and top, turn under and let the crust form again. Do this twice, allowing the crust to remain on sides and top. Bake for one hour.

DELICIOUS RICE PUDDING

½ c. rice

4 c. milk

¼ tsp. salt

½ c. raisins

2 eggs, separated

½ sugar

¼ tsp. cinnamon

1 tsp. vanilla

Cook over hot water until tender (45 minutes), the rice in 2 cups milk and salt. Last half hour, stir in raisins. Next, stir in remaining 2 cups milk, slightly beaten egg yolks, sugar, cinnamon and vanilla. Cook for 5 minutes, stirring occasionally. Carefully fold in stiffly beaten egg whites. Pour into casserole or pan and bake for 30 minutes at 350°.

CHERRIES DELIGHT

1 ½ c. shifted flour
1 cube butter

2 tsp. sugar

Mix together and press in 9 x 13-inch cake pan. Bake 20 minutes at 350°. Cool.

Filling:

8 oz. pkg. cream cheese, softened
1 c. powdered sugar
½ pt. whipping cream

1 tsp. vanilla
1 can pie filling

Mix together cream cheese, powdered sugar and vanilla. Beat whipping cream, fold into cream cheese mixture. Spread over crust. Easily pour can of pie filling over this (cherry, blueberry, peach, apple). Keep refrigerated until ready to serve.

APPLE NUGGET COBBLER

6 c. (6 large) sliced, peeled apples
½ c. raisins
½ c. chopped nuts

½ c. sugar
2 tbsp. flour
1 tsp. cinnamon

Topping:

10 oz. can Hungry jack flaky biscuits
¼ c. sugar

½ tsp. cinnamon
¼ c. butter or margarine, melted

Heat oven to 375°. In ungreased 9-inch square or 12 x 8-inch baking dish, arrange apples, raisins, and nuts in layers. Combine sugar, flour and cinnamon, sprinkle over fruit. Cover pan loosely with foil. Bake at 375° for 20 to 30 minutes or until apples are almost ten-der. Remove from oven.

For topping, separate biscuit dough into 10 biscuits. Cut each into 4 pieces. Place biscuit pieces, sugar, and cinnamon in a bag; shake to coat. Arrange over hot apple mixture. Sprinkle any remaining cinnamon-sugar mixture over biscuits. Drizzle margarine over biscuits.

Return to oven. Bake, uncovered, 15 to 20 minutes or until deep golden brown.

8-MINUTE CHEESECAKE

1 (8 oz.) pkg. cream cheese, softened
1/3 c. sugar
1 c. (1/2 pt.) sour cream

2 tsp. vanilla
1 (8 oz.) container Cool whip
1 graham cracker pie crust fresh strawberries
   (for garnish)

Beat cream cheese until smooth. Gradually beat in sugar. Blend in sour cream and vanilla. Fold in whipped topping, blending well. Spoon into crust.

Chill until set, at least 4 hours. Garnish with fresh strawberries.

LAYERED BANANA PUDDING

1/3 c. all-purpose flour
2/3 packed brown sugar
2 c. milk
2 egg yolks, beaten
2 tbsp. butter or margarine

1 tsp. vanilla
1 c. heavy cream, whipped
4 to 6 firm bananas, sliced
chopped walnuts

In medium saucepan, combine the flour and brown sugar; stir in milk. Cook and stir over medium heat until thickened and bubbly. Cook and stir 1 minute more. Remove from heat. Gradually stir about 1 cup hot mixture into egg yolks. Return all to the saucepan. Bring to a gentle boil. Com: and stir for 2 minutes. Remove from heat. Stir in butter and vanilla. Cool to room temperature, stirring occasionally. Fold in the whipped cream.

Layer a third of the pudding in a 2-quart glass bowl. Top with half of the bananas. Repeat layers. Top with remaining pudding. Sprinkle with nuts, if desired. Cover and chill at least 1 hour before serving.

BEST BREAD PUDDING

5 slices day-old bread
2 Tbsp. butter or margarine
½ c. moist raisin
¼ tsp. salt

½ c. sugar
3 eggs, beaten
3 c. milk, scaled
¼ tsp. cinnamon

Toast bread and spread with all the butter while hot. Arrange toast in a buttered 13 x 9 x 2-inch baking pan. Sprinkle with raisins. Stir the salt and all but 2 tablespoons of the sugar into the eggs. Add milk and stir to mix well. Pour over the toast and allow to stand for 10 minutes. Press toast lightly down into milk occasionally so that toast soaks up most of the milk mixture. Mix cinnamon with remaining 2 tablespoons sugar and sprinkle over top.

Place dish directly on oven rack. Bake in a moderate oven (350°) for about 25 minutes or until a pointed knife inserted in center comes out clean and top is an appetizing brown. Serve warm. Yields 5 to 6 servings.

MAMA'S RICE PUDDING

1/3 c. raw rice
¼ tsp. salt
½ c. sugar

1 qt. milk, scaled
2 tbsp. butter
½ c. raisins

Combine rice, salt and sugar in casserole dish. Add scalded milk. Stir to mix and dot with butter. Place in 300° oven and bake for 1 1Z2 hours, until rice is very tender, and milk is thick and creamy.

Stir carefully with fork every 15 minutes for the first hour, turning under any brown crust and scraping down at the edges. Serve hot or cold. Yields 4 servings.

CREAMY CHOCOLATE FROSTING

¼ c. butter
3 sq. (3 oz.) unsweetened chocolate
1/3 c. milk, scalded

2 ¼ c. confectioners' sugar
¼ tsp. salt
1 tsp. vanilla

Place butter and chocolate in top of double boiler and heat over boiling water until melted. Pour the hot milk over sugar and salt and stir until completely dissolved. Add chocolate mixture and stir to blend.

Beat, while still hot and thin, with a wooden spoon until of the proper consistency to spread. Add vanilla when mixture begins to thicken. Spread on cake when thick and creamy.

115

CHOCOLATE BUTTERCREAM FROSTING

1/3 c. soft butter or margarines
1/8 tsp. salt
3 c. confectioners' sugar

3 (1 oz. each) sq. unsweetened
chocolate, melted
¼ milk
1 ½ tsp. vanilla

Beat butter, salt and 1 cup confectioners' sugar until light and fluffy. Blend in melted chocolate. Then add rest of sugar, alternately with milk and vanilla.

Mix until smooth and creamy. Add more sugar to thicken or milk to train frosting, if needed, for good spreading consistency.

GLOSSY WHITE ICING

1 1/8 c. sugar
1/3 c. water
2 egg whites
Pinch of salt

¼ tsp. cream of tartar
3 tbsp. confectioners sugar
1 tsp. vanilla

In saucepan, stir sugar and water over low heat. Turn egg whites into mixing bowl; add salt. Beat to a foam, then add cream of tartar and beat until stiff with a wire whisk, gradually adding the confection- ers sugar as you beat. Mixture should have moist, shiny peaks when all sugar is beaten in.

When boiling sugar and water syrup, cook to 236°. Pour slowly, but continuously, over the egg whites while beating. Continue beating until cold. Stir in vanilla.

Variation:

Baltimore Icing: Substitute 1 teaspoon rum flavoring for vanilla. Fold in ½ cup chopped raisins, 3 thinly sliced, light, moist figs and ¼ cup chopped pecans.

SEVEN-MINUTE ICING

1 egg white
3 Tbsp. cold water
1/8 tsp. cream of tartar
¾ c. sugar

dash of salt
½ tsp. vanilla
glycerine

Put first five ingredients in top of double boiler over boiling water. Upper pan should not touch surface of water. Beat with rotary beater 7 minutes or with an electric beater 4 minutes or until icing stands in peaks.

Remove from heat. Set top of double boiler over cold water and add vanilla and 8 drops of glycerine. Continue beating until icing stands in shiny peaks stiff enough to hold shape.

Spread on cake immediately. Frosts two 8-inch layer cakes.

LEMON FROSTING

¼ c. soft butter
¼ tsp. grated lemon rind
¼ c. lemon juice

1 tbsp. cream
3 ½ confectioner's sugar

Mix all ingredients except sugar. Add sugar last, a little at a time, until a velvety-smooth consistency is obtained.

CREAM CHEESECAKE

2 sticks margarine, softened
1 stick butter, softened
1 (8 oz) pkg. cream cheese
3 c. sugar

6 eggs
3 c. all-purpose flour
2 tsp. vanilla

Grease and flour 10-inch tube pan. Beat together margarine, butter and cream cheese on medium speed until well mixed. Gradually beat in the sugar and continue beating for 5 minutes. Add eggs, one at a time, beating well after each addition. On low speed, beat in flour until well blended. Stir in vanilla.

Bake in 325° oven for 1 hour and 20 minutes. Cool cake in pan on wire rack for 15 minutes. Remove cake from pan to wire rack to cool completely. Dust with confectioners' sugar, if desired.

BEST EVER CHEESECAKE

1 ¼ c. graham cracker crumbs

1/3 c. butter or margarine, melted

¼ c. sugar

Filling/ Topping:

2 (8 oz. each) pkg. cream cheese, softened

2 eggs, lightly beaten

2/3 c. sugar, divided

2 tsp. vanilla extract, divided

pinch of salt

1 c. (8 oz.) sour cream

In a bowl, combine the graham cracker crumbs, butter and sugar; mix well. Pat evenly into the bottom and up the sides of a 9-inch pie plate. Chill.

For filling, beat cream cheese and eggs in a mixing bowl on medium speed for 1 minute. Add 1/3 cup sugar, 1 teaspoon of vanilla and salt. Continue beating until well blended, about 1 minute. Pour into crust. Bake at 350° for 35 minutes. Cool for 10 minutes.

For topping, combine the sour cream and remaining sugar and vanilla in a small bowl. Spread evenly over cheesecake. Return to the oven for 10 minutes. Cool completely on a wire rack. Refrigerate 3 hours or overnight.

PETITE CHERRY CHEESECAKES

2 (8 oz.) pkg. cream cheese, softened

¾ c. sugar

2 eggs

1 Tbsp. lemon juice

1 tsp. vanilla

24 vanilla wafers

1 (21 oz.) can Comstock cherry pie filling

Beat first 5 ingredients until light and fluffy. Place vanilla wafers in foil-lined cups. Fill cups 2/3 full with cream cheese mixture.

Bake at 375° for 15 or 20 minutes; no longer. Top each one with 1 tablespoon pie filling. Chill. Makes 2 dozen.

Beverages, Microwave & Misc

Beverages, Microwave & Miscellaneous

EGGNOG

4 egg yolks
4 tbsp. honey
2 c. milk

nutmeg and cinnamon to taste
4 egg whites

In a bowl, beat the egg yolks until light. Slowly beat in the honey, milk, and seasonings. Whip egg whites until stiff and fold in carefully. Chill. Pour into glasses and serve.

COLD GRAPEFRUIT NOG

2 eggs
2 Tbsp. sugar

2 c. cold grapefruit juice
orange slices (for garnish)

Beat eggs with sugar until light and fluffy. Beat in grapefruit juice. Garnish with orange slices. Serve immediately.

HOT ORANGE JUICE NOG

2 eggs
¼ c. sugar

1 c. orange juice
2 c. scaled milk

Beat eggs with sugar until sugar is dissolved. Beat in orange juice. Whisk in hot milk. Serve immediately.

SPRINGTIME PUNCH

2 c. sugar
2 ½ c. water
1 c. fresh lemon juice (3 to 4 lemons)

1 c. fresh orange juice (2 to 3 oranges)
1 (6 oz) can frozen pineapple juice
concentrate, thawed
2 qt. ginger ale, chilled

In saucepan, bring sugar and water to a boil. Boil for 10 minutes; remove from the heat. Stir in the lemon, orange and pineapple juices. Refrigerate.

Just before serving, combine with ginger ale in a large punch bowl. Makes 16 to 20 servings.

SPARKLING FRUIT PUNCH

1 c. orange juice
¼ c. lemon juice
1 (6 oz.) can unsweetened pineapple juice
1 (5 ½ oz.) can apple juice

1 (12 oz) can lemon lime flavored soda, chilled
lime slices and mint sprigs (for garnish)

Combine orange, lemon, pineapple and apple juices. Chill for 1 hour, then add soda.

Put ice cubes into 4 tall glasses. Pour mixture over ice cubes. Garnish each glass with a lime slice and mint sprig.

HONEY CITRUS COOLER

½ c. boiling water
2 tea bag
¼ c. honey
1 ½ c. cold water
½ c. each lemon and orange juices

1 (12 oz) can lemon lime flavored soda, chilled
lemon halves and maraschino cherries
(for garnish)

Pour boiling water over tea bags. Steep for 5 minutes. Remove tea bags. Stir in honey. Add cold water and fruit juices. Chill for 1 hour.

Put ice cubes into 4 tall glasses. Add soda to tea mixture; pour over ice cubes. Garnish each glass with lemon half and maraschino cherry skewered on a toothpick, if desired.

QUICK BLENDER BREAKFAST

½ c. orange juice

½ c. milk

1 banana, cut up

1 egg

1 scoop vanilla ice cream

In blender container, add all ingredients. Cover. Blend just until smooth. If desired, serve with additional scoop of ice cream. Yields 2 servings.

SPICY CITRUS COOLER

2 tea bags or 2 tsp. tea leaves

½ tsp. whole cloves

1 cinnamon stick

2 c. boiling water

1 qt. (4 c.) grapefruit juice

6 oz can frozen orange juice concentrate

Place tea, cloves and cinnamon in tea pot. Pour boiling water over tea mixture. Cover. Let stand about 10 minutes.

In 2-quart nonmetal container, combine grapefruit juice and orange juice concentrate. Remove tea bags and strain spices from tea; pour into juice mixture. Chill.

Serve over ice, stirring to combine. Garnish as desired. Yields 6 (1-cup) servings.

CHOCOLATE DIPPED FRUIT

3 sq. (3 oz.) semi-sweet chocolate

Assorted Fresh Fruit:

Pineapple, cut in 2-inch chunks fresh
    strawberries

1 ½ tsp. shortening

oranges, peeled and sectioned

In a small saucepan, melt chocolate and shortening over low heat. Use paper toweling to pat the fruit dry. Dip the fruit pieces into melted chocolate. Chocolate does not need to completely cover fruit.

Place the fruit on waxed paper-lined baking sheets. Chill until chocolate is set. Cover with plastic wrap. Chill until serving time.

DAIRY DELICIOUS DIP

1 (8 oz.) pkg. cream cheese, softened
½ c. sour cream

¼ c. sugar
¼ c. packed brown sugar
1 to 2 Tbsp. maple syrup

In a small mixing bowl, combine cream cheese, sour cream, sugars, and syrup to taste. Beat until smooth. Chill. Serve with fresh fruit.

CHICKEN SALAD SANDWICHES

1 (4 oz.) container whipped cream cheese
with chives
¼ c. thinly sliced celery
2 Tbsp. sweet pickle relish

½ tsp. Worcestershire sauce
2 c. cooked, cubed chicken
6 slices whole wheat bread lettuce leaves

In mixing bowl, stir together cream cheese, celery, relish, and Worcestershire sauce. Stir in chicken until well combined.

Place lettuce leaves on bread. Spread 3 of the bread slices with the chicken filling. Top with remaining bread slices.

Sandwiches can be wrapped in moisture vapor-proof wrap and stored for up to a week in freezer. Do not freeze lettuce leaves.

CHOCOLATE PLUNGE

2/3 c. light corn syrup
½ c. whipping cream

1 (8 oz.) pkg. semi-sweet chocolate

Microwave corn syrup and cream in large microwavable bowl on High 1½ minutes or until mixture comes to boil. Stir in chocolate until completely melted. Serve warm as a dip with fresh fruit, cookies or pretzels.

SPICY PECANS

½ c. butter

3 Tbsp. steak sauce

6 dashes Tabasco sauce

4 c. pecan halves

Cajun seasoning

Melt butter on a large baking sheet in a preheated 200° oven. Add steak sauce and Tabasco; stir in nuts. Spread nuts out on baking sheet and bake for I hour. Stir often while baking.

Drain on paper towels and sprinkle with Cajun seasoning. Store in airtight container.

SUGARED WALNUTS

2 c. water

4 c. English walnut halves

½ c. light brown sugar, firmly packed

vegetable oil

salt to taste

In a large pan, bring water to a boil. Add walnuts and boil for 1 minute. Drain nuts and rinse in very hot water; drain again. Place warm nuts in a bowl and add sugar. Stir until sugar is melted.

In a heavy skillet, heat 1 inch of oil to 320° on a candy thermometer. Cook 2 cups of nuts at a time for 3 to 4 minutes. Do not overcook. Drain on paper towels. Store in airtight container.

POPCORN BALLS

1 c. sugar

1/3 c. light molasses

1/3 c. water

¼ tsp. salt

2 tsp. butter

2 qt. popped corn

Put sugar, molasses, water and salt into a saucepan. Cook slowly until the sugar dissolves then cook more rapidly to 250° or until it forms a hard ball when ½ teaspoonful is dropped into cold water. Stir in butter. Pour syrup over popped corn, stirring continuously.

While it is still quite warm, but can be comfortably held in the hands, form into balls. Makes 1 dozen 4-inch balls.

CARAMEL CORN

6 c. popped corn
1 c. mixed nuts
2/3 c. sugar
1/3 c. light corn syrup

1/3 c. margarine
¼ tsp. salt
1 tsp. vanilla
¼ tsp. baking soda

Spray 4-quart bowl with cooking spray. Add popped corn and nuts, toss.

In 1-quart bowl, combine sugar, corn syrup, margarine, and salt. Microwave at High 2 to 3 minutes or until mixture boils, stirring well after each minute. Microwave at High 3 to 5 minutes or until small amount of syrup dropped into very cold water separates into threads which are hard and brittle. Stir in vanilla and baking soda.

Quickly pour over popcorn mixture. Toss to coat well. Micro- wave at High 2 minutes. Stir mixture and turn out onto waxed paper- lined tray to cool. Store in tightly covered container. Makes 7 cups.

CARAMEL CORN

½ c. light Karo Syrup
2 c. light brown sugar
2 sticks margarine
1 tsp. salt

1 tsp. vanilla
½ tsp. soda
6 qt. popcorn

Place first 4 ingredients in saucepan. Bring to a boil. Boil 5 minute, stirring constantly. Do not overboil. Turn off burner. Stir in vanilla. Add soda and stir again. Pour over popcorn. Stir to coat all as much as possible.

Spread in 9 x 13 x 2-inch pan. Bake at 250° for 40 minutes. Stir every 10 minutes to coat evenly.

Lay wax paper on counter and spread popcorn out to cool. Separate clumps so it dries individually When cooled, bag in plastic bags.

ONE BOWL CHOCOLATE FUDGE

2 (8 sq. each) pkg. semi-sweet chocolate
1 (14 oz.) can sweetened condensed milk

2 tsp. vanilla
1 ½ chopped walnuts

Microwave chocolate and milk in large microwavable bowl on High 2 to 3 minutes or until chocolate is almost melted, stirring half- way through heating time. Let sit until chocolate is completely melted. Stir in vanilla and walnuts.

Spread in foil-lined 8-inch square pan. Refrigerate for 2 hours or until firm. Cut into squares. Makes 4 dozen pieces.

For Rocky Road Fudge: Add 1 cup marshmallows with vanilla and walnuts.

Index

Cakes, Cookies & Desserts

Beverages, Microwave & Misc

Making The Right Food Choices

A Guide to healthy cooking and eating

People are more concerned than ever about making the right choices when it comes to eating. Once primarily concerned with weight and calories, now consumers want to know more about what they are putting into their bodies. Their concerns include a number of diet related topics such as cholesterol, fat, fiber, sodium, as well as calorie intake.

Fundcraft Publishing has gathered important nutritional information to help consumers eat smart. The following pages include topics such as nutrient content claims, health claims and the new food label and how this information can play a role in your family's diet and overall good health.

The role of fat in your diet

Fat consumption has been linked to heart disease, obesity, some types of cancer and gall bladder disease. Many public and private health authorities now recommend that Americans strive to reduce their intake of dietary fat.

The problem that confronts so many people now is how to translate these recommendations for a reduced fat diet to their everyday menu. Basically, this means selecting foods which are low in fat or fat free more often. Choosing vegetables and fruits, cereals and grain products, fish, lean meats and low-fat dairy products will help reduce your daily intake of fat.

Not all fats are created equal and not all fats are bad. Cholesterol and saturated fats are the hardest on your heart, while mono-saturated and poly-unsaturated fats are the easiest. Here's how to recognize all four in your diet:

CHOLESTEROL is a fatty substance found in animal foods including meat, poultry, fish, egg yolks, milk, cream, cheese, butter and other dairy products. Foods derived from plants such as fruits, vegetables, grains and nuts contain no cholesterol at all.

SATURATED FATS are primarily contained in animal foods including red meat and whole milk dairy products. Saturated fats can also be found in certain types of oils, notably coconut and palm and palm kernel oils, which are used in commercially baked goods. It's a good idea to cut down on foods high in saturated fats and to make substitution whenever possible.

MONO SATURATED FATS are not considered harmful to your heart, and new research suggests they may actually reduce your blood cholesterol level and, thus, your risk of cardiovascular disease. This type of fat is found in olive oil, and in certain plant foods including avocados.

POLYUNSATURATED FATS also tend to reduce blood cholesterol levels. It's the kind of fat you find most typically in sunflower, corn, soyabean and safflower oils.

Decreasing Your Fat Intake

You can lower your cholesterol level and decrease your risk of heart disease by cutting down on your fat consumption. Here are some ways:

- Avoid fried foods; bake or broil.
- Choose lean meats; cut off the fat before cooking.
- Avoid luncheon meats (hot dogs, bologna).
- Eat sparingly of sausage and bacon.
- Remove skin from poultry (before cooking, if possible).
- Steam vegetables.
- Use half the fat (oil, margarine, butter, lard, shortening, mayonnaise) called for in recipes.
- Use less than 1 teaspoon margarine or butter on bread, hot cereals, vegetables.
- Use low-fat salad dressings; limit other salad dressings to 1 tablespoon.
- Season with herbs, lemon, vinegar, onion, garlic, tomato products.
- Thicken sauces, soups with a mixture of corn starch (or flour) and cold water.
- For snacks, choose fruit, vegetables, whole grain bread/cereals/ crackers.
- Choose low-fat milk products such as buttermilk, 2% fat milk, non-fat dry milk powder and skim milk.
- Use lean pieces of meat instead of fatback as seasoning for beans, peas, greens.

The following pages provide information on how to reduce fat when making selections from the various food groups.

Fats and Oils

Some of these foods are high in vitamins A or E, but all are high in fat and calories.

SERVINGS PER DAY:

No more than a total of 5-8, depending on your caloric needs.

SERVING SIZE:

1 tsp. vegetable oil or regular margarine
2 tsp. diet margarine
1 Tbsp salad dressing
2 tsp. mayonnaise or peanut butter
3 tsp. seeds or nuts
1/8 of medium avocado
10 small or 5 large olives

Choose from:

Vegetable oils and margarine with no more than 2 gms of saturated fatty acids per tablespoon—canola, corn, olive, safflower, sesame, soyabean, sunflower.
Salad Dressings and Mayonnaise with no more than 1 gm of saturated fatty acid per tablespoon.

- Use fats and oils sparingly and use the ones lowest in saturated fatty acid and cholesterol.
- Use hydrogenated shortening sparingly and choose made from vegetable fat. They are lower in saturated fatty acid then those made from animals/vegetable fat blends.
- Use cooking styles that add little or no fat to food and ask for them when eating out.
- Replace saturated fat with more healthful substitutes. For example, when your own recipe calls for butter, lard, bacon, bacon fat or chicken fat, use margarine that contains no more than 2 gms of saturated fatty acids per 1 tablespoon, or unsaturated vegetable oil.

Using Vegetable Oils

The liquid vegetable oils or margarine that contain no more than 2 gms of saturated fatty acid per tablespoon, can be used in many ways in cooking that requires the use of fat. For e.g.:

- To brown lean meats and to pan or oven-fry fish and poultry.
- To sauté onions and other vegetables for soup.
- In cream sauces and soups made with skim milk.
- In whipped or scalloped potatoes with skim milk added.
- For making hot breads, pie crusts and cakes.
- For popping corn and making cocktail snacks.
- In casseroles made with dried peas or beans.
- In browning rice and for Spanish or curried rice.
- In cooking dehydrated potatoes and other prepared foods that call for fat to be added.

Fats and Oils

Animal fat tends to be higher in saturated fat than vegetable oils, which are generally higher in polyunsaturated fats. Vegetable shortening and margarine (see "Dairy and egg products") that have been hardened by hydrogenating contain varying amounts of saturated fat, depending on the brand. Only animal fats contain cholesterol. Amounts given are for 1 tablespoon.

Fats	Calories (grams*)	Total Fat (grams)	Saturated (milligrams)	Cholesterol
Animal fats, 1 tbsp				
Beef fat	116	12.8	6.4	14
Chicken Fat	115	12.8	3.8	11
Lard	116	12.8	5.0	12
OILS				
Vegetable oils, 1 tbsp				
Canola	124	14.0	1.0	0
Corn	120	13.6	1.7	0
Cottonseed	120	13.6	3.5	0
Olive	119	13.5	1.8	0
Peanut	119	13.5	2.3	0
Safflower, 70% linoleic	120	13.6	5.2	0
Soyabean	120	13.6	2.0	0
Sunflower, 60% linoleic	120	13.6	1.4	0
Mixed (mostly soybean, Some cottonseed)	120	13.6	2.4	0
Palm	120	13.6	6.7	0
Palm Kernel	120	13.6	11.1	0

Breads, Cereals, Pasta and Starchy Vegetables
Low in Fat and Cholesterol High in B Vitamins, Iron and Fiber

Servings Per Day:
6 or more

Serving Size:
> 1 slice bread
> ¼ cup nugget or bud-type cereal
> ½ cup of hot cereal
> 1 cup cooked rice or pasta
> ¼ – ½ cup starchy vegetables

Choose From:
Breads and rolls—
> Wheat, rye, raisin or white bread
> English muffins
> Frankfurter and hamburger buns
> Water (not egg) bagels
> Pita bread
> Tortillas (not fried)

*Crackers and snacks—
> Animal, graham, rye crackers
> Soda, saltine, oyster crackers
> Matzo
> Fig bar, ginger snap, molasses cookies
> Bread sticks, melba toast
> Rusks, flat bread
> Pretzels, (unsalted)
> Popcorn (see "Fats and Oils" for preparation)

*Many kinds of crackers and snacks are now available with no added salt or unsalted tops. Some are high in saturated fatty acids, so read the labels.

Quick breads—
Homemade using margarine or oils low in saturated fatty acids, skim or 1% fat milk, and egg whites or egg substitutes (or egg yolks within limits) biscuits, muffins, cornbread fruit breads, soft rolls pancakes, French toast, waffles

Hot or cold cereals—
All kinds (granola-type may be high in fat or saturated fatty acids)

Rice and pasta—
All kinds (pasta made without egg yolk)

Starchy vegetables—
Potatoes, corn, lima beans, green peas winter squash yams, sweet potatoes

Soups—
Chicken noodle, chowders, minestrone, onion, split pea, tomato-based seafood

If you use any egg yolks in cooking quick breads, be sure to count them in your daily allowance.

Cereals, pasta, and rice cooked without salt are lower in sodium than instant or ready-to-eat types of these food

Most soups are high in sodium, and some are high in fat. When buying soups, read labels and choose those low in sodium and fat. You can also make your own soups and control both sodium and fat.

Vegetables and Fruits
High in Vitamins, Minerals and Fiber; Low in Fat, Calories and Sodium… Contain no Cholesterol

SERVINGS PER DAY:
5 or more

SERVING SIZE:
1 medium-size piece of fruit or ½ cup fruit juice
½-1 cup cooked or raw vegetables

CHOOSE FROM:
All vegetables and fruits except coconut. Olives and avocados should be counted as fats (see Fats and Oils section). Starchy vegetables are listed with Breads, Cereals, Pasta and Starchy Vegetables because they are similar in calories per serving to the other foods in that group.

- Enjoy plenty of fruits and vegetables. If you are watching your weight, these foods will give you vitamins, minerals and fiber with few calories. Be sure to include sources rich in vitamins C & A
- Check the labels for sodium content of canned vegetables.

VEGETABLES

Vegetables can be made more tempting by adding herbs and spices. For example, these combinations add new and subtle flavors:

- Rosemary with peas, cauliflower and squash
- Oregano with zucchini
- Dill with green beans
- Marjoram with Brussels sprouts, carrots and spinach
- Basil with tomatoes

Start with a small quantity (1/8 to 1/2 teaspoon to a package of frozen vegetables), then let your own taste be your guide. Chopped parsley and chives, sprinkled on just before serving, also enhance the flavor of many vegetables.

Try cooking vegetables in a tiny bit of vegetable oil, adding a little water during cooking if needed, or use a vegetable oil spray. Only 1 to 2 teaspoons of oil is enough for a package of frozen vegetables that serves four. Place in a skillet with tight cover season and cook over a very low heat until vegetables are done.

Table For Cooking Vegetables

Vegetable	Ways to Prepare	Cooking	Time
CELERY	Scrub thoroughly. Cut off leaves and trim roots. Slice into desired lengths.	Cook covered in small amount of boiling water or in consomme.	10-15 mins.
CORN	Remove husks and silks from fresh corn. Rinse and cook whole.	Cook covered in small amount of boiling water; or cook uncovered in enough boiling salted water to cover ears.	6-8 mins.
EGGPLANT	Wash if skin is tough, pare. Cut in ½ inch slices.	Dip in beaten egg, then in fine dry breadcrumbs. Brown slowly on both sides in hot oil. Season.	Approx. 4 mins
MUSHROOMS	Wash; cut off tips of stems. Leave whole or slice.	Add to melted margarine in skillet, sprinkle with flour and mix. Cover and cook slowly, turning occasionally.	8-10 mins
OKRA	Wash pods; cut off stems. Slice or leave whole.	Cook covered in small amount of boiling salted water.	8-15 mins
PARSNIPS	Wash thoroughly; pare or scrape. Slice lengthwise or crosswise.	Cook covered in small amount of boiling salted water.	15-20 mins
PEAS, Green	Shell and wash.	Cook covered in small amount of boiling salted water.	8-15 mins
SPINACH	Cut off roots and wash several times in lukewarm water, lifting out of water as you wash.	Cook covered without adding water. Reduce heat when steam forms. Turn often while cooking	3-15 mins
TOMATOES	Wash ripened tomatoes.	Cook slowly covered, without adding water.	10-15 mins
ZUCCHINI	Wash; do not pare. Slice thin.	Season and cook covered in margarine for 5 mins. Uncover and cook till tender turning slices.	10 mins total

A "Quick;" Summary Of

DILL Both leaves and seeds of dill are used. Leaves may be used as a garnish or to cook with fish. Leaves or the whole plant may be used to flavor dill pickles.

FENNEL Has a sweet, hot flavor. Both seeds and leaves are used. Seeds may be used as a spice in very small quantity in pies and baked goods. Leaves may be boiled with fish.

MARJORAM May be used both green and dry for flavoring soups and ragouts, and in stuffing for all meats and fish.

TARRAGON Leaves have a hot, pungent taste. Valuable to use in all salads and sauces. Excellent in tartar sauce. Leaves are pickled with gherkins. Used to flavor vinegar.

CURRY POWDER A number of spices combined to proper proportions to give a distinct flavor to such dishes as vegetables, meat, poultry and fish.

CHIMES Leaves are used in many ways. May be used in salads, cream cheese, sandwiches, omelets, soups and fish dishes. Mild flavor of onion.

SAGE Used fresh and dried. May be used in poultry and meat stuffing's; in sausage and practically all meat combinations; in cheese and vegetable combinations, as in vegetable loaf, or curry. The flowers are sometimes used in salads.

CARAWAY Seeds have a spicy smell and aromatic taste. Used in baked goods, cakes, breads, soups, cheese and sauerkraut.

PAPRIKA A Hungarian red pepper. Bright red in color. May be used in all meat and vegetable salads, in soups, both cream and stock. As a garnish for potatoes, cream cheese, salads or eggs.

BASIL Aromatic odor, warm, sweet flavor, used whole or ground. Used with lamb, fish and vegetable dishes.

OREGANO Whole or ground, strong aromatic odor, used with tomato sauces, pizza and veal dishes.

BAY LEAF A pungent flavor. Available as whole leaf. Good in vegetable and fish soups, tomato sauces and juice. Remove before serving.

GINGER An aromatic, pungent root, sold fresh, dried or ground. May be used in pickles, preserves, cakes, cookies, puddings, soups, pot roasts.

CHERVIL Aromatic herb of carrot family, like parsley but more delicate. Used fresh or dry in salads, soups, egg and cheese dishes.

SHALLOTS Small type onion producing large clusters of small bulbs. Used like garlic to flavor meats, poultry, sausage, head cheese.

VINEGAR Low percentage natural acid, generally acetic acid. Used as a preservative for all pickling of vegetables and fruit. To give zest or tangy flavor to salad dressings, for meat, fish and vegetable sauces. Different kinds are wine vinegar, white vinegar, cider vinegar, tarragon vinegar.

Milk Products
High in Protein, Calcium, Phosphorus, Niacin, Riboflavin, Vitamins A and D

SERVINGS PER DAY:
2 or more for adults over 24 years and children 2 – 10 years; 3 – 4 for ages 11 – 24 and women who are pregnant or breast-feeding

SERVING SIZE:
    1 cup skim, 1/2% or 1% fat milk 1 cup nonfat or low-fat yogurt
    1 oz. low-fat cheese or 1/2 cup low-fat cottage cheese

CHOOSE FROM:
    Milk products with 0-1% fat:
    Skim milk
    1/2 – 1% fat milk
    Nonfat or low-fat dry milk powder
    Evaporated skim milk
    Buttermilk made from skim or 1% fat milk
    Nonfat or low-fat yogurt
    Drinks made with skim or 1% fat milk and cocoa (or other low-fat drink powders)

Low-fat cheeses:
    Dry-curd, skim or low fat cottage cheese, natural or processed cheeses with no more than 5 grams of fat per ounce.

- Skim, ½% fat 1% fat milk all provide the same nutrients as whole milk and 2% fat milk. But they are much lower in fat, saturated fatty acids, cholesterol and calories.
- If you're used to whole milk products, you may find it easier to make the change slowly to lower fat foods. Try 2% fat milk first. Then, when you're used to that, move to 1% fat milk. That will make it much easier if yo decide to change to skim milk.

141

Meat, Poultry and Fish
High in Protein, B Vitamins, Iron and Other Minerals

SERVINGS PER DAY:
No more than 6 oz. cooked lean meat, poultry or fish

SERVING SIZE:
3 oz. cooked (4 oz. raw) lean meat, poultry or fish

Here are some examples to help you judge serving sizes of meat, poultry and fish. A 3-ounce portion equals:

- the size of a deck of playing cards
- 2 thin slices of lean roast beef (each slice 3" x 3" x 1/4")
- 1/2 of a chicken breast or a chicken leg with thigh (without
- skin)
- 3/4 cup of flaked fish

CHOOSE FROM:
Fish (fresh, frozen, canned in water or rinsed)
*Shellfish
    Chicken (without skin) Cornish hen (without skin)
    Turkey (without skin)
    Turkey, ground
**Lean beef (from the round, sirloin, loin)
    Lean or extra lean ground beef
    +Lean ham
    Lean pork (tenderloin, loin chop)
    Lamb (except rib)
    Veal (except commercially grown)
    ++Wild game (rabbit, venison, pheasant, duck without skin)
*Shrimp and crayfish are higher in cholesterol than most other types of fish, but lower in fat and
  saturated fatty acids than most meats and poultry.
*Buy "choice" or "select" grades of beef rather than "prime."
+Ham and Canadian bacon are higher in sodium than other meats.
++Domesticated versions of game (duck and goose) are not as lean as wild game.

- Organ meats are very high in cholesterol. However, liver is rich in iron and vitamins and a small serving (3 ounces) is okay about once a month.
- Trim off all the fat before cooking meat. Drain or skim off fat from cooked meats before using juices in stews, soups, gravies, etc.
- Remove the skin and fat under the skin from poultry pieces before cooking. If you're roasting a whole chicken or turkey, leave the skin on to keep the bird from getting too dry while roasting. Then remove the skin before carving and serving the meat.
- Select whole turkeys that have not been injected with fats or broths.
- Frozen dinners and entrees may also fit into the plan. Look for those that are made specially for low-fat, low-cholesterol, low-sodium diets.
- One cup serving of cooked beans, peas, or lentils, or 3 ounces of soy-bean curd (tofu), can replace a 3-ounce serving of meat, poultry or fish.

Eggs
High in Protein, B Vitamins, Iron and Other Minerals

SERVINGS PER WEEK:

3 to 4 egg yolks a week may be eaten (egg whites are not limited).

- Because of their cholesterol content (213 mg per yolk), limit your eggs and egg yolks to no more than 3 to 4 per week. Be sure to count any egg yolks used in cooking and in store-bought foods in your total for the week.
- Use two egg whites, or one egg white plus 2 teaspoons of unsaturated oil, in place of one whole egg in cooking. You can also use cholesterol-free commercial egg substitutes.
- Eat only cooked eggs and egg whites—not raw

Desserts

A healthy, well-balanced diet can include desserts.

It's important to select your desserts carefully keeping nutrition in mind.

CHOOSE:
Desserts low in saturated fatty acids, cholesterol and calories. For a special treat, share a dessert portion with someone.

FIRST CHOICES:
(low in fat and saturated fatty acids)

     Fruit—fresh, frozen, canned or dried
     Low-fat yogurt with fruit
     Crackers and cookies (as listed in the Breads section)
     Angel food cake
     Frozen low-fat or non-fat yogurt
     Sherbet or ice milk
     Flavored gelatin
     Water ices or sorbets

SPECIAL OCCASIONS ONLY:
(higher in fat and calories)

     Homemade desserts (cakes, pies, cookies, puddings) made with margarine or is low in saturated fatty acids, skim or 1% fat milk and egg whites or egg substitutes (or egg yolks within limits). Store-bought desserts—many are now made with unsaturated oils and are either low-fat or non-fat. Be sure to read ingredients lists

A Six Month Plan

Reducing fat and cholesterol in your family's diet may not be as easy as you think. Many foods once thought to be staples of a well-balanced diet are loaded with fat and cholesterol. Here's a simple six-month plan to help reduce fat and cholesterol in your family's diet:

MONTH ONE:
- When purchasing meat, select lean, well-trimmed cuts of beef or pork.
- When cooking, use vegetable oil or softened margarine instead of lard or butter.
- Replace two red meat meals each week with poultry or fish meals.

MONTH TWO:
- Continue recommendations from month one.
- Switch from whole milk to 2%
- Eat two fewer eggs each week.
- Cut your consumption of high-fat foods such as bacon, cream, cold cuts, ice cream, cakes, pies, and other desserts.

MONTH THREE:
- Continue recommendations from first two months.
- Avoid non-dairy creamers.
- Limit organ meat meals to two per week.
- Cut down on use of cheddar cheese and cream cheese.

MONTH FOUR:
- Continue all previous recommendations.
- When recipe calls for two eggs, use egg whites and only one egg yolk.
- Limit intake of meat, fish, poultry to 8 oz. (cooked weight) per day.
- When ordering salad in a restaurant, ask for the dressing on the side, then use sparingly. Make dressings at home using safflower, corn or sunflower oils.

MONTH FIVE:
- Continue all previous recommendations.
- Switch from 2 % milk to 1% skim milk
- Limit your consumption of high fat foods such as bacon, cold cuts, cheese, etc.
- Limit fried foods to one serving per week.
- Eat only low-fat variety cheese.

MONTH SIX:
- Continue all previous recommendations.
- Eat no more than three egg yolks per week.
- Replace five red meat meals with fish or poultry, or high protein vegetables.
- Limit organ meat meals to one per week.
- Limit your intake of meat, fish or poultry to 4 oz, cooked weight per day.
- Prepare and eat poultry without skin.

Managing A Well-Balanced Diet

There are several components to managing a well-balanced diet and reducing your intake of fat is only part of the story. A diet that is high in sodium or low in fiber or one that lacks variety may not be well-balanced.

Read on for some good information on how to manage your diet so that it remains healthy and well-balanced.

BREAD, CEREALS AND GRAINS

Whole-grain breads and cereals are important sources for carbohydrates, iron and vitamins. For maximum benefits remember:

- Purchase whole-grain bread made from stone-ground flour first.
- Next, purchase 100% whole-wheat or other grain bread.
- If you decide to purchase white bread, be certain it is enriched.
- Dark bread means nothing. Most dark breads contain less or no whole grains—just molasses for coloring.
- High-fiber breads are usually lower in calories.
- Whole-grain flour may be used in bread and roll recipes.

CEREALS

- Whole-grain cereals are most nutritious.
- Puffed cereals are low in fat and salt.
- Granola is usually high in fat, salt and sugars.
- Oatmeal is the best choice of cereals.

OTHER GRAINS

- Select whole-grain, brown rice first. Converted rice comes in a distant second. Minute rice and instant rice are lowest in nutrients.
- Pasta is made from a wheat called durum. Durum won't rise so it is refined into a flour called semolina. From this, macaroni, spaghetti, and other shapes are formed. These are all nutritious and high in protein.

Increase Your Fiber Intake

Dietary fiber is the term used for several materials that make up the parts of plants that your body cannot digest. Fiber is classified as soluble or insoluble. The AHA eating plan suggests that you eat foods high in both types of fiber. Fruits, vegetables, whole grain foods, beans and legumes are all good sources of dietary fiber.

TO INCREASE FIBER INTAKE

WITH GRAINS

- Eat whole grains instead of white rice, grits, mashed potatoes and other refined starches.
- Buy baked goods and crackers where the first ingredient on the label is a whole grain.
- Add bran, whole grains, nuts to casseroles, soups, ice cream, yogurt. Coat vegetables, meats, baked products with them.
- Snack on whole grain cereals, popcorn, crackers.

WITH DRIED PEAS AND BEANS

- Use dried, cooked peas or beans in place of all or part of meat in casseroles, salads, soups and meals.

WITH FRUITS AND VEGETABLES

- Eat a fresh fruit or vegetable salad at least 2-3 times a week.
- Eat vegetables and fruits with skins on when possible.
- Choose fruit for dessert.
- Eat baked potatoes (with skin) in place of mashed potatoes.
- Eat fresh fruit and vegetables in place of juice. Drink plenty of water.
- Choose snacks of dried or fresh fruits, berries, fresh vegetables.
- Steam vegetables until crisp and tender.

Low-Fat Eating Begins With Grains

Enjoy more grains! This is a painless secret to cut fat, control weight and improve hearth. Believe it or not, you need at least six servings of bread, cereal, pasta and other grains each day.

- GRAINS ARE LOW IN FAT. Grain foods are packed with carbohydrates which contain less than half the calories of fat.
- GRAINS ARE A GOOD ENERGY SOURCE. Complex carbohydrates are our best source of fiber, and you'll feel satisfied when you eat.
- GRAINS FILL YOU UP. Because grain foods are an excellent source of fiber, you'll feel satisfied when you eat plenty of grain foods. That reduces the temptation to eat higher-fat foods.

Carbohydrates have less than half the calories of fat; therefore, you can eat more than twice as much for the same amount of calories.

TO FILL UP AND SLIM DOWN

TRY THESE SUGGESTIONS:

- Make pasta your main course three times a week.
- Eat a bowl of cereal anytime day or night.
- Grab a bagel or low-fat muffin for the commute.
- Pack a pita pocket or bagel in your purse or briefcase to ease morning hunger pains.
- Serve oriental noodles with fresh vegctables.
- Eat a breadstick or a piece of French bread.
- Snack on crackers, pretzels or fig bars.
- Roll up pancakes with fruit jam or puree.
- Sprinkle a tortilla with cinnamon and enjoy anytime.

CALORIE COUNTER
CANDIES, SNACKS AND NUTS

Calories

Almonds	12 to 15	93
Cashews	6 to 8	88
Chocolate Bar (nut)	2 ounce bar	340
Coconut (Shredded)	1 cup	344
English Toffee	1 piece	25
Fudge	1 ounce	115
Mints	5 very small	50
Peanuts (salted)	1 ounce	190
Peanuts (roasted)	1 cup	800
Pecans	6	104
Popcorn (plain)	1 cup	54
Potato Chips	10 medium chips	115
Pretzels	10 small sticks	35
Walnuts	8 to 10	100

DAIRY PRODUCTS

American Cheese	1 cube, 1¼ inch	100
Butter or Oleomargarine	1 level Tbsp.	100
Cheese (blue, cheddar, cream, Swiss)	1 ounce	105
Cottage Cheese (uncreamed)	1 ounce	25
Cream, light	1 Tbsp.	30
Cream, whipped	1 Tbsp.	25
Egg White	1	15
Egg Yolk	1	61
Eggs (boiled or poached)	2	160
Eggs (scrambled)	2	220
Egg (fried)	1 medium	110
Yogurt (flavored)	4 ounces	60

DESSERTS

Cakes:

Angel Food Cake	2" piece	110
Cheesecake	2" piece	200
Chocolate Cake, iced	2" piece	445
Fruit Cake	2" piece	115
Pound Cake	1 ounce piece	140
Sponge Cake	2" piece	120
Shortcake with fruit	1 avg. slice	300
Cupcake, iced	1	185
Cupcake, plain	1	145

Pudding:

Bread Pudding	½ cup	150
Flavored Puddings	½ cup	140

Pies:

Apple	1 piece	331
Blueberry	1 piece	290
Cherry	1 piece	355
Custard	1 piece	280
Lemon Meringue	1 piece	305
Peach	1 piece	280

CALORIE COUNTER
DESSERTS (Cont.)

Calories

Pumpkin ....1 piece 265
Rhubarb...................................1 piece 265
Ice Cream:
    Chocolate Ice Cream.................$\frac{1}{2}$ cup.........................200
    Vanilla Ice Cream...................$\frac{1}{2}$ cup.........................150
Miscellaneous:
    Chocolate Eclair, custard ....1 small 250
    Cookies, assorted...................1, 3-inch dia..................120
    Cream Puff..........................1..............................296
    Jello, all flavors...................$\frac{1}{2}$ cup.........................78

BEVERAGES AND JUICES

Chocolate Malted...........................8 ounces.......................450
Cocoa (all milk)...........................8 ounces.......................235
Cocoa (milk & water).......................8 ounces.......................140
Coffee (black/unsweetened)...0

BREADS AND FLOUR FOODS

Baking Powder Biscuits ....1 large or 2 sm...............129
Bran Muffin.......................1 medium.....................106
Cornbread.........................1 small square...............130
Dumplings.........................1 medium......................70
Enriched White Bread..............1 slice.......................60
French Bread......................1 small slice.................54
French Toast......................1 slice......................135
Macaroni and Cheese...............1 cup........................475
Melba Toast.......................1 slice.......................25
Noodles cooked....................1 cup........................200
Pancakes (wheat)..................1, 4-inch.....................60
Raisin Bread......................1 slice.......................80
Rye Bread.........................1 slice.......................71
Saltines..........................1.............................17
Soda Crackers.....................1.............................23
Waffles ....1............................216
Whole Wheat Bread.................1 slice.......................55

BREAKFAST CEREALS

Corn Flakes.......................1 cup.........................96
Cream of Wheat....................1 cup........................120
Oatmeal...........................1 cup........................148
Rice Flakes.......................1 cup........................105
Shredded Wheat....................1 biscuit....................100
Sugar Krisps......................$\frac{3}{4}$ cup.........................110

FISH AND FOWL

Bass..............................4 ounces.....................105
Brook Trout.......................4 ounces.....................130
Crabmeat (canned).................3 ounces......................85
Fish Sticks.......................5 sticks or 4 oz.............200
Haddock (baked)...................1 fillet....................158
Haddock (broiled).................4 ounces (steak)............207

CALORIE COUNTER
FRUITS

Apple (raw)	1 small	70
Banana	1 medium	85
Blueberries (frozen/unsweetened)	½ cup	45
Cantaloupe Melon	½ melon large	60
Cherries, fresh/whole	½ cup	40
Cranberries (sauce)	1 cup	54
Grapes	1 cup	65
Dates	3 or 4	95
Grapefruit (unsweetened)	½	55
Orange	1 medium	70
Peach (fresh)	1	35
Plums	2	50
Tangerine (fresh)	1	40
Watermelon	1" slice	60

MEATS

Bacon (crisp)	2 slices	95
Frankfurter	1	155
Hamburger (avg. fat/broiled)	3 ounces	245
Hamburger (lean/broiled)	3 ounces	185
Ham (broiled/lean)	3 ounces	200
Ham (baked)	1 slice	100
Lamb Leg Roast	3 ounces	235
Lamb Chop (rib)	3 ounces	300
Liver (fried)	3 ½ ounces	210
Meat Loaf	1 slice	100
Pork Chop (med.)	3 ounces	340
Pork Roast	3 ounces	310
Pork Sausage	3 ounces	405
Roasts (Beef)		
Loin Roast	3 ½ ounces	340
Pot Roast (round)	3 ½ ounces	200
Rib Roast	3 ½ ounces	260
Rump Roast	3 ½ ounces	340
Spareribs	1 piece, 3 ribs	123
Swiss Steak	3 ½ ounces	300
Veal Chop (med)	3 ounces	185
Veal Roast	3 ounces	230

SALADS AND DRESSINGS

Apple and carrot (no dressing)	½ cup	100
Chef Salad/reg. oil	1 Tbsp.	160
Chef Salad/mayonnaise	1 Tbsp.	125
Chef Salad/ French, Roquefort	1 Tbsp.	105
Cole Slaw (no dressing)	½ cup	102
Fruit Gelatin	1 square	139
Potato Salad (no dressing)	½ cup	184
Waldorf (no dressing)	½ cup	140
Boiled Dressing	1 Tbsp	28
French Dressing	1 Tbsp	60
Mayonnaise	1 Tbsp	110

Food Guide Pyramid
A Guide to Daily Food Choices

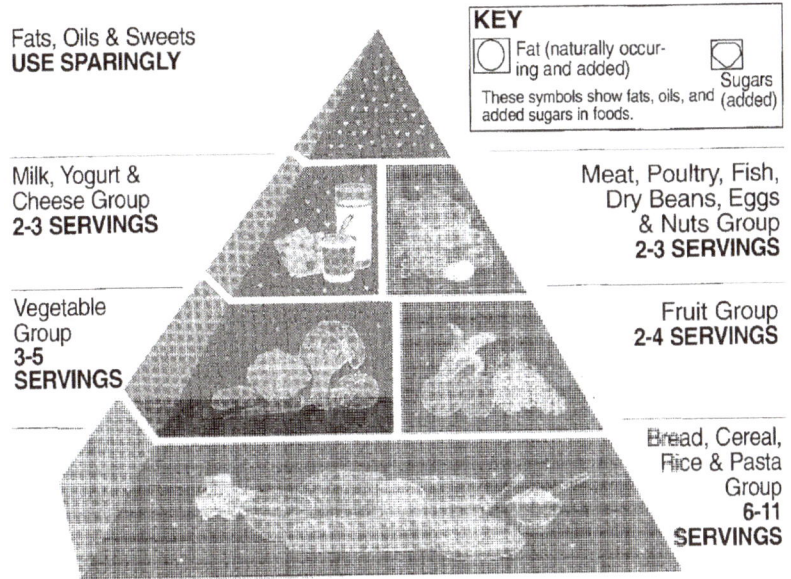

Fats, Oils & Sweets
USE SPARINGLY

KEY
○ Fat (naturally occurring and added)
◇ Sugars (added)
These symbols show fats, oils, and added sugars in foods.

Milk, Yogurt & Cheese Group
2-3 SERVINGS

Meat, Poultry, Fish, Dry Beans, Eggs & Nuts Group
2-3 SERVINGS

Vegetable Group
3-5 SERVINGS

Fruit Group
2-4 SERVINGS

Bread, Cereal, Rice & Pasta Group
6-11 SERVINGS

HOW TO USE THE DAILY FOOD GUIDE

What counts as one serving?

Breads, Cereals, Rice and Pasta

1 slice of bread

½ cup of cooked rice or pasta
½ cup of cooked cereal
1 ounce of ready to eat cereal

Vegetables

½ cup of chopped raw or
    cooked vegetables
1 cup of leafy raw vegetables

Fruits
1 piece of fruit or melon wedge

Milk, Yogurt and Cheese

1 cup of milk or yogurt

½ to 1 ounce cheese

Meat, Poultry, Fish, Dry Beans, Eggs and Nuts

2-1/2 to 3 ounces of cooked
    lean meat, poultry or fish
Count ½ cup of cooked beans,
    or 1 egg or 2 tablespoons of
    peanut butter as 1 ounce of
    lean meat (about 1/3 serving)

Fats, Oils and Sweets

Limit calories from these especially
if you need to lose weight.

> The amount you eat may be more than one serving. for example, a dinner portion of spaghetti would count as two or three servings of pasta.

How many servings do you need each day?

Calorie level*	about 1,600	about 2,200	about 2,800
Bread Group	6	9	11
Vegetable Group	3	4	5
Fruit Group	2	3	4
Milk Group	**2 – 3	**2 – 3	**2 – 3
Meat Group	2, for a total of 5 ounces	2, for a total of 6 ounces	3, for a total of 7 ounces

*These are calorie levels if you choose low-fat, lean foods from the 5 major food groups and use foods from the fats, oils, and sweets group sparingly.

**Women who are pregnant or breastfeeding, teenagers, and young adults to age 24 need 3 servings.

A Closer Look at Fat and Added Sugars

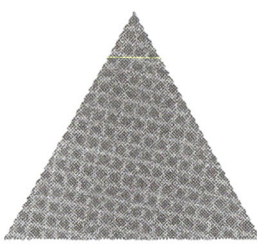

The small tip of pyramid shows fats, oils, and sweets. These are foods such as salad dressings, cream, butter, margarine, sugar, soft drinks, candies and sweet desserts. These foods provide calories, but few vitamins and minerals. Most people should go easy on foods from this group.

Some fat or sugar symbols are shown in the other food groups. That's to remind you that some foods in these group can also be high in fat and added sugars, such as cheese or ice-cream from the milk group. When choosing foods for a diet, consider the fat and added sugars in your choices from all the food groups, not just fats, oils and sweets from the Pyramid tip.

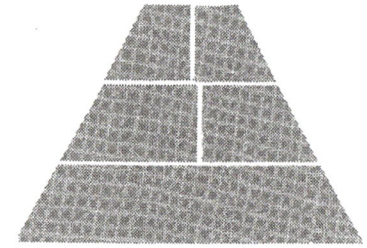

154

Managing Your Sodium Intake

Sodium is a mineral that your body needs in only very small amounts. Most Americans consume 10-15 times more Sodium than they need.

Eating too much sodium can be unhealthy for some people. It may contribute to high blood pressure. In fact, reducing the amount of sodium in your diet is an important part of treating high blood pressure.

Here are some tips to help reduce the sodium in your diet. The American Heart Association guidelines suggest consuming no more than a teaspoon of salt.

- Use less salt or no salt at the table and in cooking.
- Use herbs and spices in the place of salt. Refer to the herb and seed chart.
- Limit your intake of foods high in added sodium:
  - Canned and dried soups
  - Canned vegetables
  - Ketchup and mustard
  - Salty snack foods
  - Olives and pickles
  - Luncheon meats and coldcuts
  - Bacon and other cured meats
  - Cheeses
  - Restaurant and carry-out foods (such as French fries, onion rings, hamburgers)
- You can reduce the salt in canned vegetables by draining the liquid and then rinsing them in water before eating.
- Look for "unsalted" varieties of the canned foods and snack foods listed above. Some foods may be labeled "no salt" or "without added salt."
- Ask restaurants not to add salt to your order.
- Every bakery products and cereals can be major sources of sodium in the diet. So, read the labels of all foods carefully.

Nutrition Facts: Helping Consumers Eat Smart

Shopping and planning has never been easy. And now, with so many people concerned about the nutrient contents of foods, the choices are even tougher to make.

But now, new government regulations require food manufacturers and processors to provide dietary information on their food products. There is information on saturated fat, dietary cholesterol, fiber and other nutrients…items that relate to today's health concerns about heart disease, cancer and other diseases linked, at least in part, to diet.

One of the recent changes involves new requirements for food labels. The new food label will have a new name. now it will be called Nutrition Facts. That title will signal to consumers that the product is correctly labeled according to the new Food and Drug Administration guidelines.

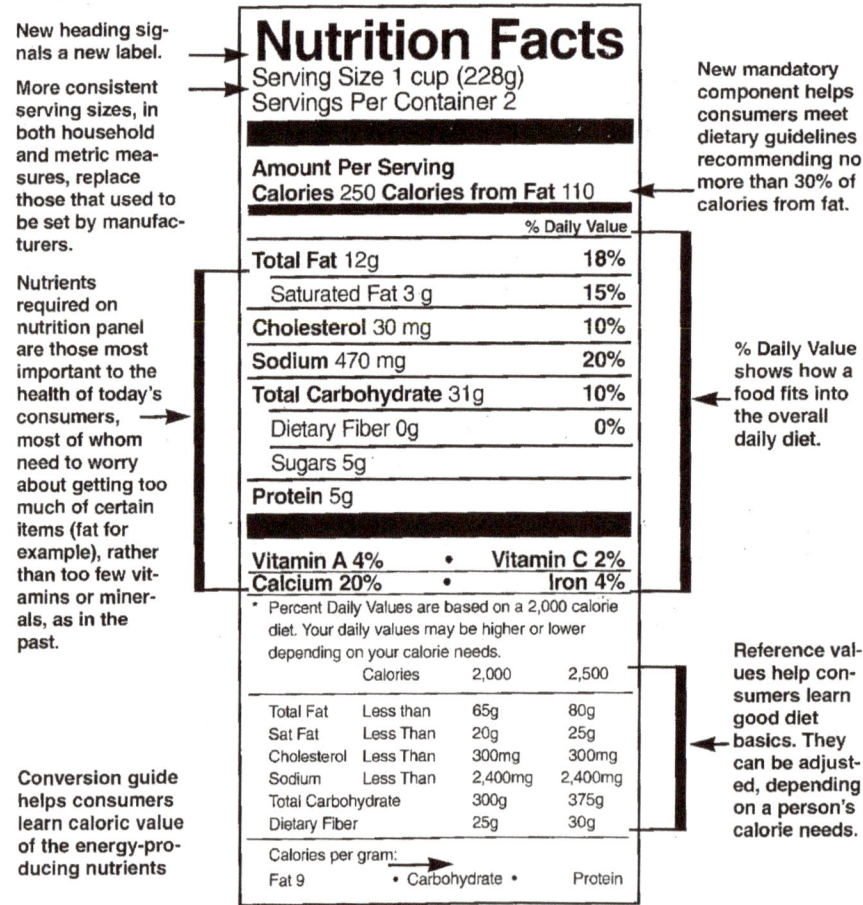

New heading signals a new label.

More consistent serving sizes, in both household and metric measures, replace those that used to be set by manufacturers.

Nutrients required on nutrition panel are those most important to the health of today's consumers, most of whom need to worry about getting too much of certain items (fat for example), rather than too few vitamins or minerals, as in the past.

Conversion guide helps consumers learn caloric value of the energy-producing nutrients

New mandatory component helps consumers meet dietary guidelines recommending no more than 30% of calories from fat.

% Daily Value shows how a food fits into the overall daily diet.

Reference values help consumers learn good diet basics. They can be adjusted, depending on a person's calorie needs.

Nutrition Facts

Serving Size 1 cup (228g)
Servings Per Container 2

Amount Per Serving
Calories 250   Calories from Fat 110

% Daily Value

Total Fat 12g	**18%**
Saturated Fat 3 g	**15%**
Cholesterol 30 mg	**10%**
Sodium 470 mg	**20%**
Total Carbohydrate 31g	**10%**
Dietary Fiber 0g	**0%**
Sugars 5g	
Protein 5g	

Vitamin A 4%	•	Vitamin C 2%
Calcium 20%	•	Iron 4%

* Percent Daily Values are based on a 2,000 calorie diet. Your daily values may be higher or lower depending on your calorie needs.

		Calories	2,000	2,500
Total Fat	Less than		65g	80g
Sat Fat	Less Than		20g	25g
Cholesterol	Less Than		300mg	300mg
Sodium	Less Than		2,400mg	2,400mg
Total Carbohydrate			300g	375g
Dietary Fiber			25g	30g

Calories per gram:
Fat 9   •   Carbohydrate •   Protein

The New Food Label—
What to Look For

The new food label can serve as an important guide to better nutrition, but only if you use it.

What should you look for?

First of all, nutrient content claims, such as "low calorie," may appear on the front label. These claims will signal—truthfully—if a food is high in nutrient that most of us need to consume less of. This may be good if you're trying to reduce your intake of calories, fat or cholesterol… or if you're trying to eat more fiber or potassium.

Likewise, health claims on some labels will point out a food's nutritional qualities that help reduce the risk of certain long-term diseases, such as heart disease or cancer. The "Nutrition Facts" will give more in-depth information to help you choose foods that fit in with a more healthful diet. Now it's easier than ever to eat healthy— just read the label.

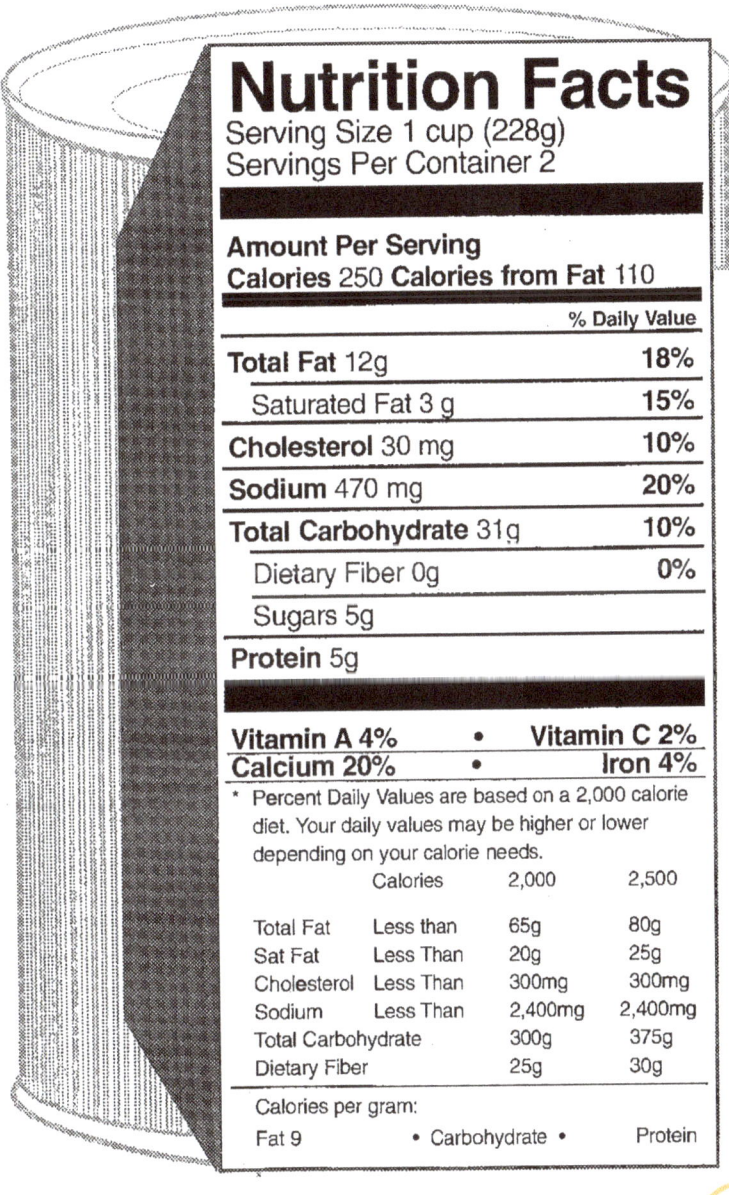

Nutrition Facts

Serving Size 1 cup (228g)
Servings Per Container 2

Amount Per Serving

Calories 250   Calories from Fat 110

	% Daily Value
Total Fat 12g	**18%**
Saturated Fat 3 g	**15%**
Cholesterol 30 mg	**10%**
Sodium 470 mg	**20%**
Total Carbohydrate 31g	**10%**
Dietary Fiber 0g	**0%**
Sugars 5g	
Protein 5g	

Vitamin A 4%	•	**Vitamin C 2%**
Calcium 20%	•	**Iron 4%**

* Percent Daily Values are based on a 2,000 calorie diet. Your daily values may be higher or lower depending on your calorie needs.

	Calories	2,000	2,500
Total Fat	Less than	65g	80g
Sat Fat	Less Than	20g	25g
Cholesterol	Less Than	300mg	300mg
Sodium	Less Than	2,400mg	2,400mg
Total Carbohydrate		300g	375g
Dietary Fiber		25g	30g

Calories per gram:

Fat 9   •   Carbohydrate   •   Protein

The Key to Healthy Eating

The amount of certain nutrients in a food now will be expressed in two ways—in terms of the amount by weight per serving and as a percentage of the Daily Value, a new nutrition reference tool. Nutrient amounts and percentages of the Daily Value describe the content of the particular food inside the package.

By using the % Dotty Values, you can easily determine whether a food contributes o lot or a little of a particular nutrient. And you can compare different foods with no need to do any calculations. A high percentage means the food contains o lot of o nutrient and a low percentage means it contains a little. Look to see whether the nutrients most of us need more of (such as carbohydrates, dietary fiber, and certain vitamins and minerals) have high percentages. Look to see whether the nutrients most of us need to limit (such as fat, saturated fat, cholesterol, and-for some people-sodium) have low percentages. The goal is to choose foods that together give you close to 100 percent of each nutrient for a day, or average about 100 percent a day over a few days.

For example, if your goal is 2000 calories a day, your total fat intake would be no more than 65 grams, the upper limit recommended for a 2000-calorie daily diet. If the food you're preparing has 16 grams of fat per serving at 25 percent, then you know that all the other foods you eat that day should total 75 percent or less of the Daily Value for total fat (or 49 grams of fat). If your daily calorie goal is 2500 calories, your daily fat would be higher.

The 2000 Calorie Basis

The % Daily values on the nutrition panel are based on 2000 calories a day. Of course, not everyone eats this amount daily; some eat more, some less. Your daily calorie needs depend on many factors, such as age, height, weight, and activity level. The 2000 calorie diet is about right for most moderately active women, teenage girls, and sedentary men. Many older adults, children and sedentary women need fewer calories a day, perhaps only 1600.

Nutrient Content Claims

In an effort to re-establish the credibility of the food label, the FDA has established criteria for the use of such terms as lite, low fat, reduced, etc. There are several core terms which are:

- Free
- low
- lean
- extra lean
- high
- good source
- reduced, less, fewer
- more
- light

Definitions for some of these terms are:
Free—item is free of nutrient.

Low—a food meets the definition for "low" if a person can eat large amounts of this item without exceeding the Daily Value for the nutrient.

Lean—used to describe the fat content: less than 10 g of fat, 4 g of saturated fat, less than 95 mgs cholesterol. Extra lean foods have less than 5 g fat, less than 2 g saturated fat and less than 95 mgs of cholesterol.

High and Good Source—focus on nutrients for which higher levels are desirable. The "high source" food must contain 20% or more of the daily value in a serving. "Good source" means it must contain 10 – 19%.

Reduced, Less, Fewer, More…—These are termed "comparison claims" and compare a nutritionally altered food to the regular or "reference" food. A relative claim must include the reference food and the percentage difference.

Light or Lite—the product contains 1/3 fewer calories or ½ the fat of the reference food…or the sodium content has been lowered by 50%.

Getting Specific

Here are examples of the meanings of some descriptive words used in food labeling.

SUGAR

Sugar Free	Less than 0.5 grams per serving.	No added sugar Without added sugar No sugar added	Processing does not increase content above the amount found naturally.
Reduced Sugar	At least 25% less sugar per serving than reference food.		

CALORIES

Calorie Free	Fewer than 5 calories per serving.	
Low Calorie	40 calories or less per serving… Or if the serving is 30 grams or less…per 50 grams of the food.	
Reduced calorie	At least 25% fewer calories per serving than reference food.	Fewer calories

CHOLESTEROL

Cholesterol Free	Less than 2 milligrams(mg) of cholesterol and 2 g of saturated fat per serving.
Low Cholesterol	20 mg or less cholesterol and 2 g or less of saturated fat per serving or per 50 g of food than reference food.
Reduced or Less Cholesterol	At least 25% less cholesterol and 2 g or less saturated fat per serving than reference food.

FAT

Fat Free	Less than 0.50 g of fat per serving.
Saturated Fat Free	Less than 0.5 g per serving and the level of saturated fatty acid does not exceed 1% of total fat.

160

Low Fat	3 g less per serving…or per 50 g of the food if serving is 30 g or less, or less than 2 tablespoons.
Low Saturated Fat	1 g or less per serving and not more than 15% of calories from saturated fatty acids.
Reduced Fat	At least 25% less per serving than reference food.
Reduced or Less Saturated Fat	At least 25% less per serving than reference food.

SODIUM

Sodium Free	Less than 5 mg per serving.
Low Sodium	140 mg or less per serving or per 50 g of food.
Very Low Sodium	35 mg or less.
Reduced or Less Sodium	At least 25% less per serving than reference food.

FIBER

High Fiber	5 g or more per serving. Foods making this claim must meet the definition for low fat or the level of fat must appear next to the high fiber claim.
Good Source of Fiber	2.5 g to 4.9 g of fiber per serving.
More or Added Fiber	At least 25% more fiber than reference food.

 **Appetizers, Relishes & Pickles**

 **Soups, Salads & Sauces**

 **Meats & Main Dishes**

 **Vegetables**

 **Breads, Rolls & Pastries**

 **Cakes, Cookies & Desserts**

 **Beverages, Microwave & Misc.**

Here's How To Use Your Thumb Index: Place thumb on black tab of the item you want to find. Flip through until a black tab appears under your thumb.

MAKING THE RIGHT FOOD CHOICES